Between Women of God

Donna Otto

HARVEST HOUSE PUBLISHERS
Eugene, Oregon 97402

BETWEEN WOMEN OF GOD

Copyright © 1995 by Harvest House Publishers
Eugene, Oregon 97402

Library of Congress Cataloging-in-Publication Data
Otto, Donna.
    Between women of God : the gentle art of mentoring / by Donna Otto.
        p.   cm.
    ISBN 1-56507-365-7 (alk. paper)
    1. Interpersonal relations.   2. Christian women.   3. Bible. N.T. Titus II, 3-5—Criticism, interpretation, etc.   I. Title.
BV4555.088   1995   95-11001
248.8'43—dc20   CIP

In tribute to
my Aunt Pat, Patricia Sayad—
an encourager to one frail girl

Dedicated to
Elisabeth Elliot Gren—
an encourager to millions

Contents

From My Heart to Yours

1. *The Classroom of the Heart* 13

2. *Is It Time for Me?* 25

3. *The Value of Vulnerability* 37

4. *Between Women of God* 51

5. *Daughters of the Heart* 69

6. *A Touch of Grace: A Visit with Elisabeth Elliot Gren* 77

7. *Caught in Comparison* 89

8. *A Unique Way of Giving* 105

9. *Frustrations and Farewells* 123

10. *Rave Reviews* 137

11. *The Fingerprint of God* 147

Epilogue: Our Privilege 159

Appendix: Mentors for Moms 167

Study Guide: A Personal Journey 185

Acknowledgments

The following people assisted in this book. There would be no book without them. I am forever grateful.

Anissa Otto
Eileen Mason
Betty Fletcher
Lisa Guest
Rick Johnson
Dick Finley
Carol Drew
The daughters of my heart

In four years anyone could get tired of hearing about the "older woman book," yet David, my husband, never expressed frustration with me, the topic, or the process. God truly meant for this man to be my husband.

From My Heart
to Yours

My house may be empty but my heart is not. The subject of this book, the relationships between older women and younger women, continues to fill me. Daily, where once I packed lunches, washed diapers, and made certain the house was tidy and dinner on the table each evening, I now look for ways to invest in the lives of younger women whom God sends to me.

The passion I have for this approach to serving God and others is significant, and I am certain far too deep to thoroughly communicate. But I want to encourage, implore, affirm, motivate, and excite you to look at what God has planned for you and the next generation. There is a younger woman for you.

Replace the sense of loneliness that comes with the later seasons of life; find a deep abiding sense of satisfaction as you pass your perspectives to starving young women just starting out on the path you are nearly completing. Recapture the memories of the past by retelling them to women who are more than interested. Give it away *now*—all you know, all you've gained, all you've lost, all the pain you experienced, all the joys you've known, all the love you have for our Lord and Savior. Give it away now, before it's too late.

Don't miss seeing the glistening eyes of a hurting young woman. Don't miss the eager ears of women needing to know you survived, and not only survived but have joy in your heart. Share with them your acceptance of each age and stage of life as a gift from God. Help them know the source to seek. Acknowledge the disappointments and broken dreams that will never be replaced.

These are what will make the next generation strong, faithful, determined, persevering. The young women in my world, daughters of my heart, have changed me, rearranged me, and brought a quality of life that I never dreamed possible. They are the Energizer battery of life.

May this task, this journey, be half as much fun for you as it has been for me.

Looking Up,
Donna Otto

Scottsdale, Arizona

*One generation shall praise
thy works to another,
and shall declare
thy mighty acts.*

—Psalm 145:4

1

The Classroom of the Heart

How many times have you heard yourself say, "If only I'd known then what I know now"? You may have been thinking of something as simple as a foolproof way to stay dry while changing a baby's diaper, or as important as how to balance a career and marriage. Somewhere along the line, nearly every woman wishes she had another woman—perhaps an older and more experienced woman—to help her negotiate the twists and turns of life.

But we live in an age where we no longer have the strong generational ties that we used to have. Grown children live hundreds of miles away from parents. Older parents are put in rest homes. We are losing our heritage, and we women are especially sensing that loss. With nowhere else to turn, we learn to dry flowers by reading magazine articles while Martha Stewart teaches us how to roast a chicken on national TV.

Life used to be different.

Woman to Woman

I grew up in cold, blustery Chicago, where we looked forward to being on the other side of that long midwestern winter. It always seemed like an eternity since we had first seen the ice build up and the city slow down because of slippery roads. Ready to welcome warmth, light, and activity back to our world, we hoped for spring when the city could get moving again. But when spring finally did arrive, our rush to get going was often stalled by too many potholes in the road—potholes we usually didn't see until our front tires fell into them! It would have been nice to have someone point them out before we got stuck.

Life has its potholes, too. But God has a way of using these cracks in the road and the unexpected lessons they can teach. Throughout my life I've been touched by women who have shown me where these potholes were or, if I already had my two front tires firmly entrenched as I sometimes did, who have told me how to get out. The lessons of life they have passed on are practical and encouraging. They are the subject matter for relationships between older and younger women—for what I think of as the classroom of the heart.

Only a few generations ago, lessons were taught in that classroom as women worked together cooking, canning, sewing, and raising children. Today we women are far removed from doing chores together. Instead we press a button to open our garage door when we leave and close it right behind us when we return. We fill our days with what seem to be good, worthwhile, and important activities, and some of them undoubtedly are just that. But we're often losing out on the better, the best, the eternal activities. We're too busy for people and for relationships characterized by intimacy and accountability. We lead fragmented lives, isolated from one another and often estranged from ourselves.

It used to be that when a baby was born, grandmothers, aunts, sisters, and neighbors all showed up to help the new mother learn to care for the baby. Women influenced one another in every area of their lives. They provided help when it was needed, hope when it was needed. In today's more mobile society, young women no longer have the support of neighbors or an extended family. In fact, the State of New Jersey has gone so far as to try to mandate that new mothers stay in the hospital longer than 24 hours after giving birth. Why? So that these women can learn about breastfeeding and caring for their newborns—lessons that were once passed on from generation to generation, from woman to woman. Now people are proposing a law so that we can learn what was once shared so naturally and easily between generations!

The busyness of our culture keeps us from passing on spiritual principles and truths as well as day-to-day lessons. And as the success of William J. Bennett's *Book of Virtues* demonstrates, people sense the loss deeply. Spiritual and moral values are virtually absent throughout our culture. The wealth of spiritual knowledge and down-to-earth wisdom to be learned from women who have walked through the experiences of life is being lost at a time when, more than ever, young women need someone to come alongside them.

My Aunt Pat

Early on I was the recipient of the kind of hands-on

caring that women of God can provide. My Aunt Pat is a hero to me and, although she died more than 26 years ago, she taught me so many things that often in the course of my day I think, "Aunt Pat taught me that!" But actually I *caught* these things from her. She lived the lessons I learned best from her.

And she captured one of these lessons in a phrase which has stuck with me all my life. Even when I was a young girl, Aunt Pat could see that I often tackled projects that were way over my head, things I could not possibly accomplish for any of a variety of reasons. That's when Aunt Pat would say, "Donna, do what you can do. Donna, are you listening? Do what you can do."

The first time I heard her say that I was trying to put a zipper (a side zipper, for you seamstresses) into a wool jumper that had a cotton lining which was too heavy for the wool. There I was, a novice seamstress working on my first sewing project. I should have been hemming a skirt, but I was charging ahead with a zipper. "Donna, do what you can do," I heard her say. She was teaching me not to get ahead of myself and so end up frustrated. Instead, I needed to do what I could at the time and be content even as I grew in my skills. It was a simple statement, but it has made a lasting impact.

Thanks to Aunt Pat, the list of what I can do is far greater than it would have been without her. She taught me how to crochet, knit, embroider, cook, and make a house a home. She was also a constant model of encouragement to me. Aunt Pat had been ill most of her adult life. She experienced 13 miscarriages, heart trouble, diabetes, and all the complications these illnesses can bring. She spent months of every year in the hospital for one reason or another and died at age 42, yet I never think of her as ill.

Never demanding or self-consumed, Aunt Pat was known for her bright smile and happy heart. Every nurse on the hospital floor looked forward to having Pat Sayad on her rounds. Aunt Pat wore her love of Christ on her hospital gown.

One wise person has observed that "nothing is easier than fault-finding; no talent, no self-denial, no brains, no character are required to set up in the grumbling business." Well, Aunt Pat had character, and she shared it with me. She helped me become a woman who sought God, and I am grateful.

As I look back, I clearly see how God has faithfully provided other older women—messengers, models, mentors—to lead me along, to show me my Lord and Savior, to share the message of His love in flesh-and-blood, hands-on ways, and to help me with the nuts and bolts of everyday living. Woman after woman helped me find Christ and thereby discover rest and hope, peace and encouragement, health and fulfillment in all that God has for me. Each one delivered her message differently, and each one was effective.

Giving Women

A description of the special type of woman that so impacted my life is nestled in the book of Titus. In this letter,

Paul is telling his younger friend Titus, his partner in ministry and student in the Lord, about the kind of relationship which we women in God's family are to have with one another. Read what he says:

> Older women likewise are to be reverent in their behavior, not malicious gossips, nor enslaved to much wine, teaching what is good, that they may encourage the young women to love their husbands, to love their children, to be sensible, pure, workers at home, kind, being subject to their own husbands, that the word of God may not be dishonored (Titus 2:3-5).

Now the lifestyle Paul describes for "older women" is in sharp contrast to the lifestyle of the women in Crete, where Titus was ministering (and, you may note, to the lifestyle of many women today!). But we'll get to that in a minute. In Crete, older women who had raised their children and were now enjoying a measure of free time customarily gathered in the afternoon to sip wine and gossip. (Is that the A.D. 65 equivalent of our going to the mall, working out, or "finding ourselves"?)

In this letter Paul reminds Titus that Christian women should be doing far different things as they grow older in their faith and as they learn to manage life more effectively. In the more mature years it is time for them to "teach what is good" and encourage younger women to "love their husbands, to love their children, to be sensible, pure, workers at home, kind, being subject to their own husbands." And how was this teaching to be done? Not through sermons.

The older woman—whose devotion to God was evident in the way she lived—would show by her very example that the Lord demands that His people be self-disciplined, temperate, chaste, respectful, clean-minded, patient, charitable, cheerful, and reverent in their behavior. An older woman who has learned when to speak and when not to and who knows what behavior reflects a genuine heart for the Lord would be a living and breathing sermon!

A Contagious Spirit

This passing on of the knowledge of God, this teaching about how to live a life that pleases Him, occurs most effectively, as in the case of my Aunt Pat, through modeling. After all, it is only natural for young people to learn from what they see. It is therefore imperative that those who are older model what is good (Titus 2:3). The godliness of older women—then and now—is far more important than any personal accomplishments the world might note. What younger women need is not someone with an impressive resumé but a true, vibrant, contagious spirituality. And this kind of spirituality is best communicated not through a sermon or a book, or even through many sermons or an entire library. Instead, this kind of spirituality is best learned when younger women see it lived out right in front of them by an older woman. It must be "caught," not taught—and that means a one-on-one, personal relationship over time.

The Concept of Mentoring

The term "mentor" comes from Homer's epic poem

19

the *Odyssey*. When King Odysseus leaves to fight in the Trojan War, he charges his trusted friend Mentor with the care of his son Telemachus and the management of the home. Mentor trained Telemachus in all the ways a father would train a son, and today we use his name to refer to a trusted counselor, guide, tutor, or coach.

In our culture, the term "mentor" tends to be associated with a specific area of knowledge. Mentors in business help new employees learn the ropes. Mentors in a special Washington D.C. program help high-risk teens complete high school. In trade unions, a person serves an apprenticeship before becoming a licensed tradesman, able then to work without supervision. My mentor when it comes to conquering the technological world of computers (the battle continues!) is 15 years my junior, but he knows his stuff and is sharing that knowledge with me. Such one-on-one attention, such personal education, is a very effective way to communicate information—as Pastor Bob Shank of South Coast Community Church in Irvine, California, realizes.

Pastor Shank defines "mentoring" as "a deliberate transfer of wisdom from one person to another."[1] He explains that mentoring is purposeful, intentional, and planned; that mentoring is a transfer of wisdom based on one's life experiences rather than the transfer of knowledge systems or behavioral techniques; and that mentoring happens in a one-on-one personal relationship through time. Mentoring calls for the commitment, focus, and single-mindedness of

---

1. Bob Shank in the *Pastor's Update Listening Guide*, February 1993, volume 36 (Pasadena, CA: Fuller Evangelistic Association, 1993), based on tape 2660.

the mentor who pours his or her life, faith, and knowledge of God into another person.

Like Pastor Shank, Dr. Howard G. Hendricks sees mentoring as "a ministry of multiplication" and "a biblically legitimate strategy for our generation."[2] When we ask ourselves the question—and all of us should—"What am I doing today that will guarantee my impact for Jesus Christ in the next generation?" being able to say that you are mentoring a younger Christian sister is an answer that will stand the test of time. Mentoring. It is indeed a biblical concept, though not a biblical word. We see it in the relationship of Priscilla and Aquila to Apollos, Barnabas to Paul, Paul to Titus, Elizabeth to Mary, and Naomi to Ruth.

Paul realized that older women—growing-in-Christ women who have lived longer and experienced more of life—have much to offer younger women. He recognized that they can and should play a key role in passing on to younger women how to live out God's truth in the day-to-day world of being a wife, mother, homemaker or career woman, and a woman whose life pleases and glorifies Him.

God values the older woman and challenges her to share her wealth of experience and the wisdom and perspective she has gained from that experience. To be growing older is not to be outdated, antiquated, or obsolete. It is being able to speak about God—His faithfulness, His redemptive powers, His willingness to provide for His children, the wisdom He offers for child-rearing, the principles

---

2. Dr. Howard G. Hendricks in *Seven Promises of a Promise Keeper* (Colorado Springs: Focus on the Family Publishers, 1994), pp. 47 and 48.

He sets forth for homemaking, the ideals and guidelines He has for marriage and living—because we've walked with Him in the valleys, the meadows, and the mountains of life.

And yes, I switched pronouns on you. The "older women" Paul talks about are you and me! They aren't other people—people stuck in the first century or people farther along in years than wherever you and I are. These directives are intended for you and me.

You may be 80 and have much to offer a 40-year-old. Or you may be 20 and find a 15-year-old looking up to you. In either situation, Titus 2:3-5 is a clarion call to women today—to older women to model; to younger women to learn. Your Creator Lord, your Almighty God, your heavenly Father, calls you in no uncertain terms to pass on to younger women your passion for Him and your commitment to His ways. How can you say no?

2

Is It Time for Me?

Perhaps you have a desire to become involved in a one-on-one relationship with another woman of God. However, you may be uncertain about your knowledge, your abilities, or your place in her life. Well, fear not, for I have reassurance, encouragement, and God's loving assurance from His Word.

Fortunately, the woman Paul describes is not necessarily a Bible scholar or an expert or professional in a particular area (although she may be one or the other or both). She has not "arrived" in the areas in which Paul calls her to be an encourager. Her marriage isn't perfect, her parenting is not perfect, her home is not perfect, her witness at the office is not perfect, and her walk with God is not perfect—but she is authentic and growing. She hasn't crossed any finish line or been pronounced "complete." She is simply spiritually older, spiritually more mature—she has been walking with the Lord longer than the women He calls her to encourage.

For this reason, a woman who has a high-school diploma and has never worked outside of her home since getting married 20 years ago has much to offer a young woman with a Ph.D. and several years of experience in the business world. The time we have spent with Christ and the fact that

He dwells within us enable us to be a beacon, an encourager, and a guide to those younger than ourselves. Furthermore, we have already found answers to questions they're now asking of God's Son and His Book.

Proverbs 31:10-31 offers a picture of such a woman. The writer begins by asking in verse 10, "An excellent wife, who can find? For her worth is far above jewels." And then the description begins. Although the details of her life (do take time to read them!) may be very different from our world, we can learn much from her example and even from the simple fact that she is described as "excellent."

The words of Proverbs and those we read in Titus are strong words. They may even cause you to have reservations about responding to God's call. And I can think of at least three other common reservations about a Titus 2 ministry that women have expressed to me over the years. Can you relate to any of them?

Older woman—that's not how I want to think about myself! Your feelings are no surprise. There's not much in our culture that commends getting older or values the status that comes with experience. In fact, our culture has a real aversion to aging (we celebrate fortieth birthdays with black crepe paper and rented hearses), we don't honor the aged (and they have so much to offer), and we don't want to admit to getting older (as if it's a secret we can keep!). In my traveling and speaking, I often say, "Will the older women in the audience please stand up?" Ninety percent of the audience may be gray-haired, but only three or four women will stand. This same aversion to aging explains why we dye our hair, have face lifts, and undergo tummy tucks. As one anonymous poet wrote in *The Grandmother's Poem:*

> *In the dim and distant past*
> *When life's tempo wasn't fast*
> *Gramma used to rock and knit,*
> *Crochet and tat, and babysit.*
>
> *Gramma now is at the gym*
> *Exercising to keep slim.*
> *Now she's golfing with the bunch,*
> *Taking clients out to lunch,*
>
> *Going north to ski and curl,*
> *And all her days are in a whirl.*
> *Nothing seems to stop or block her*
> *Now that Gramma's off her rocker.*

A touch of God's grace in my life has been my excitement about getting older. Maybe it's because of the impact of older women in my life, but as I've grown older I have always delighted in the aging process. I couldn't wait until my hair began to be salt-and-pepper gray like Mrs. Schaeffer, my fifth-grade teacher. Why this passion for aging? As I entered my middle years, the reason became crystal clear to me: I couldn't wait to return to young women what so many older women had given me.

So while most of my peers are doing what they can to hide their wrinkles, sags, poor eyesight, and gray hair, I am reveling in the aging process. I'm 50 and proud of it. I'll never hide my gray! After all, according to Proverbs 16:31,

"A gray head is a crown of glory; it is found in the way of righteousness." I want to see those slender silvery reminders of all God's seen me through, all He's taught me, and all He's given me to share with younger sisters.

Besides, have you ever noticed that there's nothing threatening about a gray-haired woman? In fact, there's something very welcoming about her, with her soft smile, gentle wrinkles, and warm bosom. Yes, as we get older, gravity takes its toll, doesn't it? But a grandmotherly bosom is a welcoming place for a younger woman to lay her head and find comfort, encouragement, and hope. As you think about all this, I hope you're beginning to feel a little bit better about the natural and God-ordained process of aging. We older women have a lot to offer!

A few years ago, when my peers were talking toning, hair color, and ways to dress so they looked younger, my dear friend and mentor Elisabeth Elliot Gren modeled for me what I always thought was right to do. She did not dye her hair, and she even changed its style to a bun. She practices what she teaches about accepting the gift of aging. She proudly wore her wrinkles and always dressed appropriately for her age. Her example encouraged me. My season was here and I could celebrate—and I still am. I like growing old!

But you may not be celebrating. You may instead share our culture's aversion to aging. If that's the case, ask God to change your perspective on aging from society's warped lack of respect to an appreciation of the rewards and special ministry opportunities that come with our later years. May you come to hear the word *older* with new ears.

Sounds like a great ministry opportunity, Donna, but I'm busy... and besides, I did the Sunday school teaching/vacation Bible school/choir/church office volunteering/committee chairing for years! At the risk of stepping on toes, let me ask you, "What are you busy with—things for today or things for eternity? Things which *you* want to do, or things which *God* wants you to do?" Be honest with yourself. You only get one chance at this business called life, and God will hold you accountable for what you do with that gift. Don't have any regrets! Let me also remind you that none of us ever retires from Christian ministry. Glorifying God, becoming conformed to the image of Christ, growing in the knowledge of our heavenly Father, serving our Lord—these and other aspects of being God's child comprise a lifelong process. So don't be resting on your laurels! And don't be wasting valuable time on things that will be dust and ashes. Be heavenbound, not earthbound, in the use of your talents, your energy, and your days on this earth.

Donna, I have time. I understand the importance of the ministry and the desperate need in today's society. I'd like to be involved, but what do I have to offer? Dear sister, for starters, you clearly have a humble, warm heart and a godly desire to serve and be used by God. That's a wonderful starting point and an ideal position from which to have an effective and life-changing (yours as well as hers) ministry to a younger woman. I know well-educated, high-powered, high-energy young women can be intimidating, but what they don't have in their life is exactly what you can offer—a reassuring presence, stories of God's faithfulness, reminders that babies don't cry/have colic/wear diapers forever, that God is greater than office politics, and that He has a special plan for your life, whatever your marital status. The list of what you can give goes on and on.

Several years ago when I addressed an audience of young women, I asked them, "Why do you want an older woman in your life?" A young woman jumped to her feet and responded, "I need someone to assure me that my three-year-old Jennifer will not be wetting her pants for the rest of her life!" This is certainly something you can give!

The tremendous news is that when God calls, He empowers. And He calls each one of us to this ministry of passing on our love for Him and knowledge of Him, of passing on to younger women how to be godly wives, mothers, homemakers, and women of God in the community, at the workplace, or in the gym. Know that He will provide. He will be with you, blessing you each step of the way as you say to Him, "Here am I. Send me." I know God will richly bless you as you bless the younger women He brings into your life.

❧ *Mentoring Moment* ❧

From the Serengeti Plain in the African country of Tanzania comes a vivid picture of the value of the older to the younger. . . .

If a newborn wildebeest does not stand up in the first ten minutes of its life, it will be abandoned. The herd has no choice but to move on, away from all-too-present predators.

The elders of the herd—not only the parents—surround the wobbly-kneed baby wildebeest, providing warmth and support in an attempt to insure that it will stand and be ready to move on.

Too often we human beings do far less for our younger ones.

God Provides

If you are still hesitating to step forward to a Titus 2 ministry, I encourage you to think about my roses. When I was growing up in Chicago, we lived in a rambling old two-story house built on a small lot typical of that dim, dark, and barren older part of the city. My mother, tutored by the next-door neighbor, worked to add a touch of brightness and color to our home. That was not an easy task in the Midwest where flowers appear for such a short time.

My mother planted two rosebushes just outside the back door. She babied those plants, clipping broken branches, dusting the bushes with powder to keep them dry, covering them in the winter, and keeping them evenly watered. For years and years, those roses in the yard meant hours of work that resulted in maybe 15 blooms (but usually fewer than half that number) each summer.

In the late seventies when my husband's work moved us to a new home in Arizona and the subject of landscaping surfaced, all these memories surfaced. I never even considered roses. "Roses?" I asked. "Never! Too much work, not enough reward." But now, 20 years later, I have more than 30 rosebushes in my gardens, each one producing too many blooms to count. In Arizona roses are easy to grow.

I am still amazed by these beautiful blooms. How is it that I, Donna Centanne, an ugly duckling kid born on the wrong side of the tracks to parents of no education, influence, or wealth and growing up in the darkness and dirt of an old part of a large city—how is it that I am here in the midst of all this beauty?

The answer is simple. I'm here and I'm blessed—by roses and so much more—because of the grace of my Sovereign God. He provides. And He alone knows where I would have ended up had He not, in acts of pure grace, provided older women in my life—women who have opened doors of beauty, hospitality, spiritual discovery, creativity, art, apparel, and so much more. "God provides" is the message of my roses to me and, I hope, to you. The Lord uses those roses to remind me of His gracious and faithful provision for me, and He can and will use you—yes, you—in the life of His younger daughters. As He provides for them through you, He will provide for you what you need to minister to them in service to Him.

Blessings on You

As the baby boomers approach their fiftieth birthdays, the number of older women in America will grow. It may be the only time in U.S. history there will be enough older women to go around. It is my prayer that they will accept God's Titus 2 challenge and freely share with younger women whatever they have learned about knowing God and living a life which pleases Him. It is also my prayer that those of us who have the opportunity right now to be older women to these baby boomers will do so—that we will reach out to them so that they will have a model for reaching out to others.

Their message in the future will be the same as your message and mine today because it is God's eternal and unchanging message. But the message we are commanded in Titus 2 to share will be communicated in a variety of ways, each reflecting the unique personality of the messenger. Your relationship with a younger Christian woman—where you find her, how you encourage her, what you do together, the thoughts and feelings you share—will look different from mine and everyone else's. But you can be confident that the ministry you have in her life will be just as valid, just as life-changing, just as important to God's kingdom as anyone else's ministry.

The book of Titus clearly tells us that we women have an important role to play in the lives of younger women, and no one else can take our place. So as you open your life and your heart to a younger woman, trust that God will use you. God may send you to an office so you can influence a younger woman there, or He may ask you to go into your local church and begin a Titus 2 group for yourself and others. He may call you to open up your life to a neighbor, a young woman at church, or the daughter of a friend. No matter what, keep walking with Him and, as Aunt Pat used to tell me, "Do what you can do." As you and I walk with God and spend time with Him, we are changed in the presence of a holy God, and we are able to be all that He desires us to be and to do all that He calls us to do.

3

The Value of Vulnerability

Have you ever noticed that the first phrase spoken by
every angel you meet in the Bible is "Fear not"? The most
familiar instance is probably when an angel of the Lord suddenly appeared to the shepherds that first Christmas night.
The darkness was broken by the angel's radiance, startling
the simple shepherds. That's when the angel said, "Fear not:
for, behold, I bring you good tidings of great joy, which shall
be to all people. For unto you is born this day in the city of
David a Savior, which is Christ the Lord" (Luke 2:10,11
KJV).

That same message applies when we begin to consider
becoming a Titus 2 woman in the life of a younger woman.
Stepping out in faith means developing a relationship with
someone new, and that means taking a risk. (Opening your
heart and your life to an older woman is just as much a risk!)

But as we've all been told: Anything worth doing
is worth doing well, and anything worth doing will cost
something. This two-part bit of wisdom certainly applies
to Titus 2 friendships between older women and younger
women. The first cost you may encounter as you obey God's
command will be overcoming your fear and taking the initial risk of beginning a new relationship.

Facing the Challenge

People deal with fear and new challenges differently. A popular option today is taking a class for whatever you're facing. You can enroll in classes to learn how to give birth, care for a newborn, cope with a toddler, encourage children in school, and deal with adolescents. You can take classes on spiritual growth or on learning how to be a witness for Christ in the workplace. My husband teaches Family Circles, a Sunday school class for about 50 young married couples at our church. The list of potentially useful classes goes on and on.

But when a young woman is struggling with a difficult situation and is certain her situation is unique, she doesn't need a class, a seminar, or a how-to manual. She needs a mature friend, and she will benefit greatly from the presence of an older woman who has walked through more of life and discovered that "this, too, shall pass." She needs a classroom of the heart. The older woman's eyes, filled with compassion, communicate understanding and care; her gentle touch offers comfort; and words learned from her own life experience provide hope and set a standard—God's standard—for the younger woman's life. In fact, the older woman's gracious ways and godly presence may be the most comforting language in the world. And yes, making that connection means taking a risk—for the older woman as well as the younger. But taking that risk, besides being an act of obedience, has benefits and blessings for both women. Let me give you an example.

The Risk of Imparting Our Lives

"My husband no longer calls me twice a day. He must not love me." When I heard my young friend, newly married, speak these words through tears, I smiled to myself. She felt rejected and unloved and was certain that this change in her husband's behavior signaled a lack of his love. I remembered well those thoughts and feelings.

But I also had a bigger-picture perspective, as any woman married longer than five years would. After all, it never fails that a man's focus changes after he's married. He first conquers his woman and then, to care for her and show how much he loves her, he goes out to conquer his world. And he usually sets aside the behaviors he used to win his wife when he wages the battle to earn a living. Does his change in behavior mean he no longer loves his wife? Certainly not! Yet his new bride often feels pushed aside.

Now when this young friend of mine picked up the phone and called me, she didn't want me to refer her to a book or a research paper on the subject of men. She didn't even want me to point her to the Bible—at least not yet. Instead, she wanted and needed a person who had experienced the same situation, felt similar pain, and persevered through it. I could do that. I didn't need to know a single resource to offer her. That's not what would help her pass through this storm of fear. All I needed to do was say, "Be not afraid" and offer her some hope—and so I did.

But I did so at some risk. Just as she took the risk of sharing her fears, I took the risk of sharing my story and myself. We both took the risk of exposing ourselves to the other.

The apostle Paul knows about this kind of risk. He wrote to the believers in Thessalonica:

> Having thus a fond affection for you, we were well-pleased to impart to you not only the gospel of God *but also our own lives,* because you had become very dear to us (1 Thessalonians 2:8; emphasis mine).

In this single sentence, Paul touches on two issues that relate to an older woman/younger woman relationship. First, he uses the phrase "fond affection," something that is fundamental to our role as older women. We must care about the women God sends. After all, they are His beloved, gifts He offers us to love and encourage, to pray for and teach. We must never regard them as trophies to be added to our display cases or evidence of a prideful obedience to Titus 2. God has entrusted these precious young women to us, and we are privileged and honored to be used by Him and to offer them "fond affection" in His name.

Second, Paul touches on the issue of authenticity and the ability to be real. We are to share not just head knowledge and book learning about life. We older women are to share "our own lives." Only in the bonds of Christian love am I comfortable sharing my weaknesses, my failures, and my ongoing struggles. That Christian love means I'll be accepted, not judged; encouraged, not belittled; lifted up, not put down. And that kind of Christian love works both ways in an older woman/younger woman relationship of the heart.

So when she called, I told my young friend how I cried and cried when David stopped calling me every day at 8:30 A.M. as he had in the years we courted. When I complained to him, his response was so logical. (Of course I did not want logic!) He said, "Why would I call you at 8:30 when you just took me to the train at 6:30?" I don't remember my answer, but I'm certain it was fraught with emotion and confusion.

I've also told younger women who were having problems with envy about the jealousy I felt toward other women in David's life—not because of anything he did or didn't say or do but simply because of my own family history. Sharing our sins, failures, and struggles like this is never easy—not for a younger woman and not for us older women.

✢ *Mentoring Moment* ✢

Excellence is willing to be wrong,
Perfection is being right.

Excellence is risk,
Perfection is fear.

Excellence is powerful,
Perfection is anger and frustration.

Excellence is spontaneous,
Perfection is control.

Excellence is accepting,
Perfection is judgment.

41

Excellence is giving,
Perfection is taking.

Excellence is confident,
Perfection is doubt.

Excellence is flowing,
Perfection is pressure.

Excellence is journey,
Perfection is destination.

An Authentic Life

But sharing our sins, failures, and struggles is the trademark of authenticity. Just as the very real Skin Horse did in its conversation with the new Velveteen Rabbit, talking about what happened to cause our hair to fall out, our eyes to drop out, or our joints to get loose is what authentic people do:

> "Real isn't how you are made," said the Skin Horse. "It's a thing that happens to you. When a child loves you for a long, long time, not just to play with, but REALLY loves you, then you become Real."
> "Does it hurt?" asked the Rabbit.
> "Sometimes," said the Skin Horse, for he was always truthful. "When you are Real you don't mind being hurt."[3]

---

3. Margery Williams, *The Velveteen Rabbit* (New York: Holt, Rinehard and Winston, 1983), pp. 4-5.

Living life, being loved, getting hurt, experiencing joys and heartaches, and knowing God in the valley, on the mountaintop, and when He's silent—these things make us real. These things make us authentic. And these things enable us to be to younger women the messengers of God, the beacons of His light, and the channels of His love that they need. Again, we can't teach what we're not. We can only teach who we are. And living a life with the Lord makes us His authentic people, prepared for the ministry He calls us to in Titus.

You might imagine how relieved this tearful young friend was to find out that she was not the only wife in the world to be disappointed by her husband; that an older woman she respected had felt unsure in her marriage; that someone else not only had experienced this same situation but had survived it; and that her husband was very normal and probably still loved her very much.

My young friend shared her own life, and I shared mine. We both exposed some of the fears of our heart. This dear woman found understanding, acceptance, and encouragement simply because I shared a little of myself and my experiences as a wife. Having done so, I could then direct her to the resources I knew about—a videotape on men and how they tick, a book on the differences between men and women, and always God's Word. First we needed to risk sharing our lives. Then came the heart-to-heart connection and the comfort that we women of God find when we grow together.

The Risk of Pointing to God's Truth

I'll never forget the time Gloria arrived at my door. She was sobbing uncontrollably. I took her in my arms and just let her cry. Her pain was very deep. Her husband had found another woman, and Gloria was embarrassed, angry, hurt, afraid, and confused. Certain she had made a mistake marrying this man, she wondered how she could tell her parents, and she didn't know what would happen to her now.

After I heard details about secret telephone calls and hidden bills, a letter from the other woman, and the scene of the confrontation, Gloria paused and said, "Donna, I know I am to forgive him—BUT!" What joy I found in being able to simply reaffirm for her that truth in her life. Her heart said, "Run from this pain," her culture said, "Dump him," but her God said, "Forgive him."

Forgiveness is a process that, unfortunately, doesn't erase the pain quickly. And as you know, it is never easy to watch someone we love undergo the kind of heartache Gloria was feeling. But such pain brings us face-to-face with the hope we find only in God. Our heavenly Father is the God of our suffering, not just the God of delightful and happy times. And our God hurts with us when we hurt. He understands our humanness, He knows our hearts, and He realizes that forgiveness is a struggle for us.

God also knows how important it is for us, His people, to draw alongside one another when our hurts run deep.

That is what Gloria needed from me—my presence, my hugs, my tears shed with her. But after we cried together for a while, she needed something else. Remember playing "Pin the Tail on the Donkey"? When it was your turn, a blindfold was placed over your eyes and you were pointed in the wrong direction so that finding the donkey was as difficult as possible. Well, I play a reverse "Pin the Tail on the Donkey" with the younger women God brings into my life. When they come to me I don't blindfold them, and I always point them in the right direction—toward God, His life-giving Word, and occasionally, when they need more help than I feel qualified to give, toward a pastor or more qualified person.

After the storm of emotion faded, Gloria realized that God called her to forgive her husband. At that point, all I did to help Gloria was to assure her of that truth which she already knew. I kept her facing in the right direction: toward God and His Word. Then, during the roller-coaster days and weeks that followed, I continued to remind her of God's truth when circumstances suggested she take a different approach to the situation, and I continued to be available to her. Sometimes her call would come late at night, and then it was often a frantic three-minute conversation that began with, "Donna, tell me again." And I did. I reminded her of God's great love and compassion and of the commands (like "Forgive") which He has instituted for our own good.

I also encouraged Gloria to do what she could do just like my Aunt Pat had encouraged me. Gloria could not make her husband turn around and be faithful. She could not change what had happened. But she could continue trying to be the best wife possible. And Gloria did the hard things. She prayed for her husband, she didn't run from the situation, and she didn't kick him out. She loved him and waited, offering him the hope of forgiveness. Each step of the way, just as when she first arrived on my doorstep, she practiced "Be not afraid," willingly risking the possibility of greater pain and further rejection from her husband. She believed that being faithful to God's Word meant letting herself be vulnerable in that way, and I stood by her side with prayer, acceptance, and love.

When a young woman like Gloria faces a difficult situation, is feeling the deep pain that life can bring, or needs an answer, that need—whatever it is—will best be met by someone who has been available to her in the past, someone who has understood her, given her the freedom to be authentic no matter how awful it looked or sounded, and accepted her whatever she was feeling. Getting that close to one another is a risk that both people take, but it's a risk which a younger woman willingly takes when she knows that a godly older woman will never blindfold her or point her in the wrong direction but will instead open her eyes to the love of Jesus and point her to her Maker and His heart of compassion.

The Rewards of Risk

The kind of closeness that God grants between women of God is the result of risk-taking. Sometimes the only way an older woman can take that initial risk is by gritting her teeth and acting out of obedience to God's command in Titus, trusting that He will be with her as she does what He says to do.

I know the first step on any journey always seems hardest. You may be unsure of the response you will receive or wonder "Was that appropriate? Am I doing the right thing?" But read what one woman wrote after taking her initial step: "Today, Tammy and I got together for the first time. I think I'll have to take off my shoes for I'm truly on holy ground. It was wonderful!" God blesses when, in obedience, we step out in faith, trusting Him to be with us.

Being a beacon of God's light and a channel of His love, being Jesus with flesh and bones for a young woman—this can look like an intimidating assignment from the outside. But like any ministry, you'll be covering this special outreach in prayer, asking God to guide you, use you, and bless the time you spend with His younger daughter. He will honor your prayers. Yes, you need to trust that God has brought this young woman into your life in response to your prayers. And yes, you need to trust the young woman as you share with her your own life and heart. But remember that you will never be in it alone. Jesus will always be there with you (Matthew 28:20). Knowing that the bond of His love exists and that He is there in the relationship with you can indeed help you risk and help you trust.

One more thing. In my Bible-study program Mentors for Moms (see Appendix), the only requirement for mentors is simply that they love Jesus. A heartfelt love for

Jesus is more than enough to encourage young women. That genuine love for Jesus also enables us to willingly take a risk for God's beloved young daughters, to extend to them "fond affection," and to be authentic with them at the same time that we allow them to be authentic with us. So be not afraid! Knowing that the Lord is at your side, boldly go out and be a Titus 2 woman to that younger woman God will bring into your life.

"Come to the edge," he said.
They said, "We are afraid."
"Come to the edge," he said.
They came.
He pushed them and
they flew.

—Guillaume Apollinaire

4

Between Women
of God

If you come to my home for dinner, especially in the winter months, you will probably find a huge apple pie for dessert. It has been a family favorite for only about 15 years because it was only then that I mastered pie-baking. (I was a late bloomer in the art.)

I have one of those dandy apple-peeling gadgets that peels and slices at the same time. I found a surefire pie-crust recipe, and that's essential. Using a pastry cloth and rolling-pin cover help immeasurably. I also settled on those green Granny Smith apples and determined the right amount of butter, flour, sugar, and cinnamon to go with them. Once the bottom crust is in the pan and the apples are in the crust, I create a design on the top crust. Sometimes the design is as simple as the letter representing the person we're celebrating. Sometimes I get a little more elaborate.

But now every pie I make—whatever the occasion—reminds me of an important lesson: "It's never too late to learn something new." And that message is certainly relevant here as you get ready to respond to God's command to become a Titus 2 woman and welcome a younger woman into your world, into your heart.

Of course these daughters of the heart (my favorite description of the young women God has placed in my life to encourage)—daughters in your church, daughters for a season, daughters of the heart whose parenting was weak, difficult daughters of the heart, faltering daughters of the heart, and daughters of your friends—are a wonderfully varied breed, and I've been blessed by a wide spectrum of them. Out of that experience come the following suggestions and how-to's for these God-ordained relationships. (For more insight into your role as a Titus 2 woman, take time to work through "A Personal Journey" at the back of this book.)

Let me also remind you of the truth of Isaiah 46:4: "Even to your old age, I shall be the same, and even to your graying years I shall bear you!" May the specific suggestions which follow, as well as this promise the Lord makes to you, encourage you in your new adventure and help you truly enjoy the younger woman God sends your way. After all, she is God's gift to you.

Making the Connection

Meeting a young woman may seem like a difficult task, and it may be harder for some of us than for others. But for everyone the first step is prayer. Ask God to bring you a daughter of the heart. Then, having begun to ask God to choreograph a Titus 2 relationship for you, open your eyes and look around. You will probably have only to look around your sphere of influence—the worlds of church, friends, office, neighborhood, volunteer work, kids' activities—to discover God's answer to your prayers. That certainly was the case for us when my husband and I met Kim.

Sent by the Lord

In 1988, David and I met Kim Moeller, and we didn't go out of our way. We met at a church committee meeting. She was lighthearted, bubbly, and adorable—and, like David, had been born and raised in Wisconsin. In our casual conversation, we discovered she was single and might be interested in serving on another committee with us. Frankly, one of the main reasons I suggested that she join us was my "Yenta" trait. (You remember matchmaker Yenta in *The Fiddler on the Roof!*) You see, there was this dear single man on that same committee . . .

As our conversation at that evening meeting ended, Kim said, "If I could ever help you in any way, let me know." Never offer to help Donna Otto because I'll always take you up on it!

A month later, I was working on a huge project that kept me from running a few necessary errands. Kim came to mind, so I phoned her. The conversation went like this:

Donna: "Hi, Kim. Remember me?"

Kim: "You bet! How are you?"

Donna: "Fine—and I'm calling to take you up on your offer to run a few errands for me."

Kim (silent for a long time and then finally): "I'd love to, but I don't have a car. I'm riding the bus these days."

Donna: "Well, we have the Old Brown Belle that we offer to anyone in need, and you're welcome to it. Come by and pick it up."

Kim (silent again for an even longer time): "Well, you see, I'm taking the bus because I can't afford to pay my car insurance. I'm disciplining myself to ride the bus as a way of getting my finances in order."

Let me break in here. Kim did not know that David and I had just been discussing what to do with our home. Since our daughter had left for college out of state, we had some empty bedrooms and so had decided to seek the Lord for someone we could help. Kim couldn't have known about our conversation or our prayer. Neither could she have known how much David and I value the kind of openness and authenticity she had just shown.

Donna (bold as usual): "How much is your car insurance?"

Kim: "$250 every six months."

Donna: "How much is your rent?"

Kim: "$250 a month."

Donna: "Well, if you came to live with us for 30 days, you would have the money for the car insurance, and you could help me a few hours a week in return."

Kim: "Really?"

Donna: "Let me talk to David tonight. We'll pray and you pray, too. I'll call you in a few days."

Honestly, our conversation was that brief, that direct and to the point. David and I discussed the matter. We realized we had only met Kim once, but decided even if she were Attila the Hun, in 30 days she would be gone!

Seven days later, Kim—with loads of stuff and her little orange car—moved into our home and into our hearts. She didn't stay a month—she stayed two years. And during that time, she truly became a daughter of my heart. We worked together, prayed together, laughed together, and had a few spats together.

During her stay, Kim worked with a financial counselor and disciplined her spending habits. When she moved into her own apartment, Kim was not only debt-free, but she had some savings for emergencies as well. We smile when we think about those money lessons and hard-earned bank accounts because when Mr. Right (actually Mr. Robert) came on the scene, he was very careful with a dollar. He might not have been as crazy about a gal in debt!

Two years after Kim moved out of our home and into her apartment, Kim and Robert were married in a lovely morning wedding in our garden. It was picture perfect, if I do say so myself.

How do you explain this kind of unexpected appearance of a daughter of the heart? Sent by God is all I can say. Of course God sends all of the various kinds of daughters of the heart. He ordains that they be in your life. But there was an extra touch of grace in Kim's arrival. I hadn't initiated the relationship, and I hardly knew her. But I will always be thankful that God had her land on my doorstep.

Sharing Skills and Interests

Here's another example of finding people to mentor right within your own sphere of influence. An excellent seamstress and a godly woman, Carol was taking an advanced class in tailoring when she met Tammy, who was not only interested in being mentored by a woman who knew everything about sewing but who, Carol saw, needed a spiritual guide as well. The two became friends because they shared an interest in sewing, but within a year Carol had introduced Tammy to Jesus Christ, and Tammy had welcomed Him as Lord of her life.

Like Carol, you probably won't have to look far for a younger woman to welcome into your life. Consider the young women God has already put within your reach, those you see regularly, and those you spend time with. Look around your neighborhood, your church, your place of employment, the clubs you belong to, and the classes you take. Chances are the person God has for you is closer than you think.

If you are a young woman just starting out in married life or mothering and want to be in relationship with an older woman, look for places in your community where older women are involved and make your presence known there. If you feel that God is calling you to get close to a particular older woman, volunteer to serve her as a way to link yourself to her. A young woman in our Family Circles group who asked, "Could I come help you with Poppa?" when David's father became ill and moved in with us has become a dear daughter of my heart. She recognized a need and offered to meet that need, I accepted, and God blessed us with a very special relationship.

But keep in mind that, just as God never forces Himself on us, we aren't to force ourselves on others. Yet know, too, that when we are faithful in prayer about the Titus 2 relationship we desire and take some common-sense steps to get in touch with that older or younger woman we want, God will respond and bring to us the one He has chosen in advance.

For example, I am absolutely certain that wherever you live and whatever church you attend, God has a young woman there waiting for you to pass on to her the godly convictions of your life. In fact, the church where you worship is the best place for you to begin this service to Christ. A house of the Lord is an excellent place to seek a woman with whom to share your lifelong spiritual walk and the lessons you've learned along the way.

Pray for the women around you as you sit in the sanctuary on Sundays. Help in the nursery and pray for the young mothers as they come in, all the while keeping your eyes and heart open for one who needs help. Go to the teacher of a young marrieds Sunday school class and offer to be an older woman to anyone whom the teacher knows needs someone to walk alongside her. Or surprise your pastor and let him or her know that you are available to encourage, advise, or give a younger woman a shoulder to cry on. Don't wait for a younger woman to take the initiative. That's your job—and let me assure you it's a wonderful job to have!

You may be able to be close to more than one young woman at a time, but be careful not to overextend yourself (maybe having a small group of women to lead at one time is your answer). You wouldn't want to miss the blessing that a Titus 2 relationship can be!

Getting to Know One Another: Asking Questions

A lot of women find asking getting-to-know-you questions difficult, and often don't know where to begin. In Mentors for Moms we've found "A Few of My Favorite Things" a good place to start when an older woman and younger woman first want to get acquainted. If using the following list feels a little awkward to you, begin by acknowledging that to your younger woman and let those words break the ice: "I hope you don't mind my referring to this list, but I really like some of the questions here and thought they would help us get to know each other better—and I really do want to get to know you." If someone said that to me, I'd do whatever she suggested!

What is your favorite . . .
(adapted from Mentors for Moms)

Color
Breakfast
Lunch
Dinner
Dessert
Time of day—and why?

Place in the house—and why?
Piece of furniture—and why?
Season of the year—and why?
Holiday—and why?

Fabric
Way to be touched
Recreational activity
TV show—and why?
Film
Flower
Book of the Bible
Verse in the Bible—and why?
Speaker—and where did
   you first hear him/her?
Musician
Song
Type of music

Radio station
Book
City or town you have
   lived in
Childhood memory
Gift you've received (list
   three)
Place to study
Way to spend money
Way to spend time
Favorite anything else
   you'd like to share

Learning to Listen

For years David has kidded me that I am a woman of two verbs: "buy" and "talk." Actually, my tendency to talk too much has been an area that I continue to ask God to change in me. I ask Him to help me listen, and I have to practice keeping quiet. When I am quiet, I find I learn more than when I'm talking. By learning to ask simple questions and then really listening to a younger woman, you will open a path of discovery between you that you will cherish.

The first time I met with Jill Goodman, we sat at a table and shared a wonderfully deep conversation. She was new to the faith and to our church, and I can still remember the moist eyes—hers and mine—as she shared her story. I quietly listened to this woman God had brought into my life through a study I was teaching. The second time we met together, we again sat at a table, but this time we shared a meal. Again, I just listened—and that's not always easy for me to do!

A wise person has said, "Silence is the mother of prayer and the daughter of a holy heart." Take it from someone who knows! Don't talk all the time. Instead, make a conscious effort to really listen to this young woman of God. Hear her words; hear her heart. In doing so, you will be a great comfort to her.

Hearing about Her Goals and Dreams

Once you've broken the ice, don't stop developing your question-asking and listening abilities! A sure way into anyone's heart is to get her talking about her goals and dreams—When you were 12, what did you dream about doing in life? What do you hope to accomplish before you die? What goals did you set for yourself this year?

As author Gil Beers observes, "A question is one of the most wonderful communications devices in the world":

Reflect back on the last three conversations you have had with someone. Did that person show a genuine interest in how you spend your day, what you like or don't like, what you think about certain matters, and what you would do if you were in a certain situation? I think it's safe to say that you have had very few persons ask you questions like these about your thoughts, your concerns, your convictions, your values, your interests, your reactions, your "heartbeat" about life. Most of us can count these kinds of conversations on the fingers of one hand and have fingers left over.

When I ask you a genuine question about your thoughts . . . your experiences, or anything else that concerns you, I extend a person-to-person invitation. . . . Remove personhood from heaven or earth and either becomes a sterile test tube devoid of love, grace, truth, peace, friendship, and a hundred other qualities that make life exciting because it is personal.

Not only will asking questions help you get to know your younger woman better, but it will also help your younger woman get to know herself better. Hearing her talk about her goals and dreams will also allow you to pray for specific issues and details in her life. At some point you can ask her about her relationship with the Lord. One of my favorite questions is, "Tell me about your personal spiritual journey." Be willing to share some of your own story. After all, she needs to get to know you, too.

As your relationship grows, don't be afraid to ask the younger woman how you can help accomplish her goals, especially in those Titus 2 areas of her walk with the Lord, her marriage, her children, and her home.

Offering Encouragement

Encouragement is one of the greatest gifts we older women can give younger women today as they struggle to be godly women, wives, mothers, homemakers, and career women in our confused and confusing society. As you get to know a younger woman, you will see some obvious and very personal ways you can encourage her in the challenges she faces and the demands she feels. To help you get started, though, consider the following ten ideas, adapted from a list I've had in my files for years.

∾ Write an encouraging letter (Paul to Timothy).

∾ Share how God has dealt with you—your personal testimony of overcoming and growth (Paul's testimony in Acts 22).

∾ Offer your supportive presence, even when you don't understand (the women at the cross). Don't withhold friendship when a sister stumbles or embarrasses you (Joseph and Mary, Paul and the Corinthians).

∾ Affirm her worth by showing kindness when she hurts (Jesus in Matthew 25—feed the hungry, visit the prisoners, clothe the naked, etc.).

∾ Compliment your younger woman on the progress she makes in the faith (1 Peter 1:22; 1 Thessalonians 1).

∾ Be available and willing to listen (Paul corresponded with the Corinthians when they needed and asked for his help).

∾ Be a cheerleader—offer celebration when the situation looks dim (Paul and Silas in prison).

∾ Jump in and help her actually complete a job (John and Peter went to Philip in Samaria, Acts 8).

~ Stand up for your sister, defending her when others disparage her (Barnabas for Paul, Acts 9).

~ Review with her the record of God's involvement in your past and present, so she can get the future into perspective (Paul to the Philippians).

❧ Mentoring Moment ❧

Simple encouragement can be extremely powerful. For me, one-line gems spoken by two of my own mentors have encouraged me again and again in times of difficulty. The first, of course, is my Aunt Pat's "Do what you can do." The second is Elisabeth Elliot Gren's "Do the next thing."

When Elisabeth Elliot's husband, Jim, and his party were speared to death by the Auca Indians in 1956, a stir was created around the world. Leaders from many nations sent words of prayer and comfort to the wives of the slain men and their children who were living in Ecuador. Through this time of pain and questioning, the best advice Elisabeth received from a friend was "Betty, do the next thing." She looked around and the next thing was not to write a book, or speak a profound word or prayer, or even to comfort someone else; the next thing to do was to change her daughter Valerie's diaper.

Sharing Books, Tapes, and Videos

Many fine materials on being a wife, mother, and woman of God are available in Christian bookstores and perhaps even in your church library. Reading a book together, listening to a teaching tape, or watching a video like

Elisabeth Elliot's *Peaceful Home* (one I heartily recommend) can be very profitable activities for you and a younger woman. When you choose a video, watch a little of it, stop the tape, and talk about what you've just seen and heard. Take notes as you watch so you can go back and refer specifically to a point that was made. Do the same with audiotapes and be sure to tackle books in bite-sized pieces, too.

One time I decided to explore a subject area that was entirely new to me, and I invited my daughter of the heart to join me. I simply said, "This is a topic I know nothing about. Do you want to learn with me?" We had a grand time. As we both learned something new, she learned more about me, too.

Setting Boundaries

How often will you meet together? Once a week? Once a month? How long will you meet when you do get together? One hour or two? How frequently will you call one another and how long will you talk when you do? Both of you will benefit when you know what to expect.

After all, if a young woman does not clearly understand who she is in your life and how she fits in, her confusion can interfere with the ministry God has called you to and the blessings He has for both of you. But if you have clearly laid out the parameters of your relationship, your young friend will not be wondering about the rules. She will be able to relax in the relationship, share herself more freely, and receive more completely all that you have to offer her.

She will also see in you a healthy example of setting bound-aries. At the same time, you will have protected yourself from feeling crowded or taken advantage of. Do you see that having these lines of communication open—right from the start—will make the relationship work better for both of you?

Taking Time to Review

Open-ended commitments are hard for everyone in-volved, so let me suggest that right at the start you set a time to evaluate your new relationship. It's usually wise to begin with a limited time frame: "Shall we meet four times and see where we are?" If you already know this young woman and sense a solid foundation for your relationship, you might say, "Let's plan to meet for six months and then reevaluate." Not having clear guidelines and a specific sched-ule for when you'll evaluate how it's going can make it hard to end the relationship. Many mentoring relationships will evolve into a "daughter of the heart" relationship, but not all of them will.

But let me also caution you about ending the rela-tionship prematurely. As I look back on my life, I see long periods of time when no growth was evident. So I encour-age you to hang on to the woman God sends you through thick and thin as long as you feel it's His will and you sense her sincere desire to learn from you. When you don't see any desire for growth or any efforts to change on the part of the young woman, and when God seems to be giving you permission to move on, it's time to end the relationship.

And that can happen more gracefully if, from the start, you've identified points along the way for evaluation.

Such preset points for review provide opportunities to go over the guidelines and boundaries you have established. If you sense your younger friend struggling or wanting more than you are able or feel comfortable giving, clear the air. By doing so, you will keep the relationship open and enable yourself to be used in her life so that she can be all God wants her to be.

Being a part of that kind of growth—being used by God in someone's life to help her be the woman He intends her to be—is truly joy unspeakable. Do you know the old hymn? "It is joy unspeakable and full of glory and the half has never yet been told." Not until we are in the presence of God will be know the full effect we have on the young women God sends our way when we make ourselves available to be used by Him.

5

Daughters of
the Heart

If you've ever met around a table for prayer, sharing, and the study of God's Word, you know what God can do when you sit across from someone with your Bible and an open heart and begin to learn together about Him and each other. I haven't done any scientific research, but my experience around a table—the comfortableness, the closeness, the ability to read and write in good light, the chance to look into another person's eyes, the warmth of a shared pot of tea—has taught me that it's an ideal setting for growing deeper with God and your daughter of the heart. I like our dining room table, but any table will work. So once you've gotten acquainted, invite your new friend to your table. Get a cup of something warm to drink, your Bibles, some paper to write on, and a box of tissues, then see what God will do when two women of God come together.

Feeding on God's Word

When my friend's grandson asked for a cookie, she quickly sliced him an apple for a snack, telling him as she did that apples would make him grow up to be big and strong. But even before Grandma finished slicing the apple,

69

three-year-old Brandt had climbed onto the counter and grabbed the cookies. "I don't want to be big and strong," he said as he darted past her, the first cookie nearly devoured. "I want to be fat and widdle."

You and I are a lot like Brandt. We often eat "cookies" and then wonder why we aren't big and strong enough to serve God as we desire. That's why I suggest you spend time studying the Bible with your daughter of the heart. I often turn to the New International Version Serendipity Bibles (call Serendipity House in Littleton, Colorado, at 1-800-525-9563). These Bibles were created for small groups (you and your young woman qualify!). Since they include discussion questions for every passage, they are very helpful tools when it comes to growing "big and strong" in the Lord.

Also look into Bible-study opportunities at your church. If nothing formal is offered, ask for some suggestions about material and do your own study with your younger woman. Christian bookstores offer a wide variety of easy-to-use study guides. Spend a morning with your younger woman looking at material together. If that sounds like more than you want to tackle, look into the Bible studies available at a larger church in your area and attend there. Also find out if Bible Study Fellowship, a national study group, is active in your community.

Remember, though, that studying God's Word together doesn't have to be tightly structured to be extremely valuable. I know two women, one in her early forties, the other in her late twenties, who met regularly for a one-year period to read and talk about the book of Isaiah. Two others went for weekly drives and memorized a passage of Scripture each week. Just reading Scripture out loud to each other or memorizing verses is a great way to grow together in Christ.

Being Faithful in Prayer

Faithful prayer is a significant element in this God-ordained relationship between a younger woman and an older woman. No one can know the vital role such prayer plays in the older woman's ministry and the younger woman's struggles. In your prayers, ask God to:

- ∾ Guide you in praying for your younger woman and increase your concern for her.
- ∾ Block the enemy's plans against her.
- ∾ Bless her and manifest His goodness in such a way that there can be no doubt that it is His goodness, not coincidence or chance.
- ∾ Strengthen every good personality trait and good desire she has, and encourage right decisions.
- ∾ Make her open and receptive to His voice and sensitive to her own personal sin and need.
- ∾ Release her from any bondage, rid her of any prejudice, and break the hold that sin or an evil habit may have on her.
- ∾ Surround her with His holy presence, and remind her of His many past mercies and His merciful intervention in new and powerful ways.

∾ Melt away any hesitation she might have about moving closer to Him.

∾ Allow her to know His great and merciful love.

(Adapted from the Mentors for Moms program)

Of course, you will also pray about the specific and daily concerns your younger woman talks about, but the areas listed above will keep you mindful of her major goals and such bigger issues as her walk with the Lord, her need for His protection, and her ability to hear His voice.

Praying Together

"I learn more from people when they are praying than any other time." These are the words spoken to me by a dear older woman in my life, and I agree wholeheartedly.

While our prayers are directed to God and for His attention and glorification, the family of God is blessed and informed as we pray aloud with one another. Your daughter of the heart will learn about you, your love for God, your level of authenticity, and most certainly the depth of your passion for the King.

A few reminders about praying together:

1. *Pray frequently*—on the phone, when you are together, and at points in your conversations when appropriate. Let her know that you believe God hears and answers the prayers of a righteous woman.

2. *Pray honestly.* Begin with confession. Be honest before God and her about your shortcomings and failures. Emphasize the fact that you believe God cares

for all areas of our lives, large and small. This will help point her toward God when she has any need.

3. *Pray in an understandable manner.* Taking your younger woman into consideration, pray in a way that will not confuse or muddle her thinking. Use simple terms and simple phrases.

4. *Pray Scripture.* Do not hesitate to read a passage of Scripture as a prayer, showing her the power of God's Word when recited back to Him.

5. *Pray when you don't have "the" answer.* Make it a habit when asked a question you do not know to stop and ask God for the answer. This pattern will reinforce your dependency on Him for all things.

Make prayer time a "Sweet Hour of Prayer," tender and transparent. It is in prayer we receive strength and courage to attend to life as God planned.

Keeping It Simple

Don't become so caught up in going deeper that you forget the life-changing effect that simple moments together can have. Remember, you don't have to be perfect to help your young woman face the challenges of her world. You will do that just by letting her into your life. For a young mother, having the freedom to get away from the kids for an hour may be all she needs to blossom. For a single or career woman, a quiet lunch together may provide the opportunity to refine your younger woman's perspective on life and refresh and encourage her in the challenges she faces.

You don't have to orchestrate deep conversations. Sometimes all a younger woman needs to see is an older woman finding satisfaction in folding a load of clothes. However, if you are working together in the kitchen or folding laundry and a subject comes up about which you would normally stop to pray—by all means, stop to pray! Sometimes you will need to make opportunities, but sometimes you just need to *take* the opportunities the Lord gives you.

Walking with the Lord

Never try to be an older woman alone. Instead, let God be part of this ministry each step of the way. Be a woman of prayer and rely on Him to bless you as you minister to His younger daughter. He will be your guide as well as your source of wisdom, patience, and love. Furthermore, through prayer and the Holy Spirit, you have total assurance of access to your daughter of the heart in every situation. I'm finding great comfort in that fact right now as, sequestered away in a cabin with no telephone so I can finish writing this book, I sense the need to communicate with a dear daughter of my heart. I can't speak to her. I can write, but a letter will take days to reach her. I have complete access to her heart through the power of prayer and the Holy Spirit. I can touch her with God's love today.

If cookies are your diet, and consequently you are still "fat and widdle," may I send you to the eternal, everlasting fountain of life for a long, deep drink of His strength and sustenance? Be big and strong, not fat and widdle.

6

A Touch of Grace

A Visit with
Elisabeth Elliot Gren

When I was in my early thirties, God sent an older woman into my life who has had a profound effect on my understanding of godliness and what can happen between women of God. When I met author Elisabeth Elliot Gren, I knew right away that she offered me a model of godliness and could teach me much. In fact, she is that kind of model to literally hundreds of thousands of women through her 29 books and five-day-a-week radio broadcast.

I'm hardly alone in thinking of Elisabeth as a spiritual mother. But perhaps because of my track record in drawing close to and learning from older women, perhaps because of my persevering nature, and perhaps because Elisabeth wanted to help me, she has been an important "older woman" to me in the Titus 2 sense of the phrase. Many years ago I asked Elisabeth if she would be willing to teach me and help me be a woman of God. I have watched her closely as she has taught other women and managed her home and her life. Moment by moment and day by day, her life truly reflects the messages she shares in her books and public appearances, and it offers many lessons to those of us who have had the opportunity to watch her up close as well as from afar.

Older Woman, Younger Woman

In 1988, Elisabeth and I had one of several discussions about the older woman of Titus 2:3-5. I was trying to come up with a way to refer to this special woman. Elisabeth suggested, "How about the WOTTs woman—the Woman of Titus Two?" Now, whenever I think of that older woman whom Paul describes in Titus, I smile and think of Elisabeth and her term straight from Scripture!

I recently asked Elisabeth what she thinks of the nineties term *mentor* as a synonym for a WOTTs woman. Pointing out that *mentor* is a broader term than we have in mind, she continued:

Anybody—man or woman—can be a mentor. I think of myself as an "older woman" because it is a biblical term. We need not limit it to chronological age. A younger woman may be more mature spiritually than a woman who is older chronologically.

I remind young women who longingly wish for an older woman in their life, "*You* are supposed to be a spiritual mother too. Spend more time asking God to qualify you to be a spiritual mother to someone. Remember, if you're 20 years old, the 15-year-old is looking up to you!"

When my next-door neighbor Ruth was 15, I was nine and thought of her as an adult. To me, she was a model of Christian womanhood—a sweet, unselfish, friendly, loving Christian girl—the next-door neighbor who paid attention to me.

"How many younger women can we take into our heart at one time?" I next asked Elisabeth.

As many as God sends! But I don't think we should go rushing around trying to gather together a group. Women sometimes tell me that I am to them what Amy Carmichael was to me, and I think, "Lord, You know that I'm not in that category. I'm not qualified for that." But that's not really my business. I keep going back to the verse where Jesus says, "You didn't choose me. I chose you." So let's be willing to be available, to be broken bread and poured-out wine for as many younger women as God puts in our path.

Interestingly, Elisabeth never met Amy Carmichael, the Irish missionary to South India who founded Dohnavur Fellowship, a refuge for children in danger. She served in India for 53 years and died in 1951 after spending the last 20 years of her life bedridden and in pain. Elisabeth got to know Amy through her books. In the preface of the biography Elisabeth wrote about Amy's life, *A Chance to Die*, Elisabeth notes, "Dohnavur became a familiar place. I knew its bungalows, its paths, its people; I breathed its air. Amy Carmichael became for me what some now call a role model. She was far more than that. . . . She showed me the shape of godliness."

❧ *Mentoring Moment* ❧

An excerpt from

"If"

by Amy Carmichael

If I belittle those whom I am called to serve,
talk of their weak points
in contrast perhaps with what I
think of as my strong points;
if I adopt a superior attitude,
forgetting, "Who made thee to
differ? and what hast thou that
thou hast not received?"
then I know nothing of Calvary love.

If in dealing with one who does not respond,
I weary of the strain, and slip
from under the burden,
then I know nothing of Calvary love. . . .

If I myself dominate myself,
if my thoughts revolve around myself,
if I am so occupied with myself I rarely have
"a heart at leisure from itself,"
then I know nothing of Calvary love.[4]

Continuing her thoughts on availability, Elisabeth said:

I have to pray that the Lord will enable me to live in such a way as to be an example to people I don't

---

4. Amy Carmichael, *If* (Christian Literature Crusade, 1992).

even know. God has given me a public ministry. That word *ministry* means "servanthood." A mother has a ministry; a wife has a ministry. You need not have a public platform. You may be ministering to those around you when you least expect it and in very simple ways. We can learn a lot just from watching godly older women who may have no idea of the impact they have on our lives.

With this in mind, I questioned Elisabeth about our relationship. "Do you see me as a Titus 2 'younger woman' in your life?" I asked. She responded:

I wouldn't, Donna, except that you tell me I am! I have to accept your testimony and the fact that you've told me that you see me as a mentor, spiritual mother, older woman, and I thank God for that privilege.

I wondered whom Elisabeth had learned things from and asked her who had been the most significant older women in her life. She replied:

Of course my mother. She was by far the most significant older woman in my life and the only person who really came to mind as belonging in this category.

The next most important woman who greatly influenced my life was Mrs. DuBose, headmistress of the school I attended in Florida. She was extremely hard on me. She was also gifted with the ability to discern potential in people. So to her I owe a great debt. She saw in me potential I would never have recognized myself, and she forced me to work on those areas. So I learned to play the piano, sing, write, speak on platform, and do things like that in my mid-teens.

Then when I was in college, an older woman was both my housemother and Sunday school teacher— Miss Cumming. She was also among the most influential. It is, however, only in retrospect that I look back and see that God, in His mercy and love, gave me a number of older women who greatly influenced my life.

A Titus 2 Ministry Today

Thinking about the state of our society and the direction it's headed, I then asked Elisabeth about the role of the older women in today's culture. Will the Titus 2 woman become even more valuable during the next 20 years?

Yes! I certainly think that when people don't have a Christian mother or have a mother who is not living as a Christian mother should, there is a great need for others to pick up that responsibility. That's why it's important that we lodge in the minds of all Christian women that they are meant to be mothers not necessarily in the biological sense but always in the spiritual sense.

We grandmothers have all this great wisdom and all this experience (she says tongue-in-cheek), "What are we supposed to do with it?" But a serious and more important question is "What does God want us to do with the information we have?"

I had a conversation with a woman who said, "I'm an available woman." I liked that term, so I said, "What do you mean by that?" She replied, "I am available when people need me. I have time to read my Bible, time to pray, time to counsel with other people."

The retirement years present us with serious temptations—to idleness, to self-indulgence, to pampering. This is a colossal waste of God-given gifts. God has given wisdom, strength, experience—and He is giving us the gift of old age. Do we think of it as a gift? These are called "the golden years," yet so many people deplore them, dread them, deny them, insisting that they are not old. Joseph Addison's hymn says, "Through every period of my life Thy goodness I'll pursue," and that is one of my prayers for myself. It is also the prayer of the psalmist who prayed, "Teach us to number our days, that we may apply our hearts unto wisdom" (Psalm 90:12 KJV).

Hearing Elisabeth's comments, I couldn't help wondering why older women aren't seeking out younger women more today. Why is there sometimes a striking difference between the older women we meet in books (in the Bible or in other accounts of great Christian women who have gone before us) and the older women we meet in real life? And so I asked Elisabeth, "Isn't the living out the life of Christ what the older woman-younger woman relationship is all about?"

I think each individual is meant to walk before God in such a way that the life of Christ in her mortal flesh is visible. In Titus 2, Paul is not talking about writing books, giving lectures, and holding Bible classes. He is saying, "Teach"—which means "to show." It's "show and tell," and it's more showing than it is telling. Everyone knows that what we are is far more influential and powerful than anything we ever say. But if we have things to say, then people have a right to look for evidence that we live by our words.

But do other older women often feel inadequate and even afraid to respond to God's call to them in Titus 2?

If we are going to do something for God, we first need to acknowledge our weakness and our inadequacy. Practically everybody in the Bible who ever did anything for God had an argument with Him—"You picked the wrong man, the wrong tribe. What am I going to do? Nobody is going to listen to me." There's Jeremiah, Gideon, David, Moses. Mary didn't quarrel with God, but she did ask, "How can this be?" and was overwhelmed by the tremendous gift that was being given to her. Then, of course, she was humble enough just to receive it and be thankful.

Nothing is going to make us more soberly aware of our inadequacy than spiritual responsibility. But let us not excuse ourselves. As Moses was saying, "Who am I?" God was saying, "It doesn't matter who you are. I AM is sending you."

If anyone thinks she's qualified and would make a great spiritual mentor, then I'd say she's not qualified!

Each of us should be directed primarily toward God—doing what He says, living the way He describes the Christian life, and trusting that God, in His own way, in His sovereign plan and working in our lives, will bring the older woman and younger woman into contact with each other when He sees the need for that. Daily we should be saying to Him, "I'm yours, Lord. Show me what I can do for You today."

The Bible's "Older Woman"

Knowing the importance of the Titus teaching for relationships between women of God, I was curious and asked Elisabeth what other passages of Scripture support—if not command—this special ministry:

Psalm 145:4 builds on this Titus 2 concept—"One generation shall praise Thy works to another, and shall declare Thy mighty acts."

First Timothy 5 talks about helping the widows. That description of widows is what any Christian woman was expected to have been doing all her life.

Elisabeth makes a good point. In 1 Timothy 5:3-10, we read about older Christian women who have practiced piety in regard to their own family, fixed their hope on God, prayed day and night, lived above reproach, earned a reputation for good works, showed hospitality to strangers, washed the saints' feet, helped those in distress, and devoted themselves to good works. These women certainly sound like good candidates for a Titus 2 ministry to younger women!

The Word Made Flesh

Some concepts covered by Scripture are rather abstract. I asked Elisabeth if there weren't some things that can only be taught by passing them on, one woman of God to another.

You are talking about the great principle of the Word made flesh, and it certainly is true that the word of Christ has to be made flesh in each of us. At the same time, the flesh has to become the word. When a woman is in love, for instance, she not only wants the presence of her lover, but she wants his word, too. She wants him to write a note with a rose that says, "I love you." She wants to hear him say, "I love you." So flesh has to become word and word has to become flesh. That is the truth of Scripture. And that—God's Word that has become flesh and flesh that has become word—is what women are looking for.

Amen and amen! And thank you, Elisabeth!

7

Caught in Comparison

Mixed-up priorities, busyness with the wrong things, inattention to the Scriptures, the absence of prayer and quiet time with the Lord, a lack of fellowship—all these things can interfere with our journey toward Christian maturity (and they do!). But I am convinced by the number of women I have met that one problem stands above the others, and that is the *deadly sin of comparison*.

You know how it goes:

"If only I were as creative as she is . . ."
"If my husband were as kind to me as hers is to her . . ."
"If I knew the Bible the way she does . . ."
"If I had her blonde hair . . ."
"If I were as thin as she is . . ."
"If I had her brains . . ."

We make comparisons like these at all stages of life. Whenever we place ourselves next to other women, we can find an endless number of areas where we see ourselves falling short. Nothing is a bigger source of discouragement, poor self-image, or an ungrateful spirit than this tendency to measure our own worth by what we think we see in others.

The temptation to make comparisons is something you and I need to pay special attention to as we become Titus 2 women. The enemy will definitely use this tendency to establish roadblocks on your journey toward becoming the woman God wants you to be—the woman He wants you to be as you reach out to others. It may also become a source of difficulty if your younger woman begins to compare herself to you. Let's look at some of the ways comparisons can interfere.

Comparison Keeps You from Recognizing the Truth

When my friend or the woman I know only from a distance, if at all, becomes the standard I feel I must measure up to, I am no longer focusing on God's standards for me. I miss His truth. And I miss Jesus Christ Himself, who is the purest standard for each one of us.

Have you ever been to an amusement park with a young child? You head for the roller coaster, ready to pay for two tickets, when you see the colorful sign that reads, "Children must be this tall to ride the Mighty Loop." The smiling clown extends an arm to indicate that magical height, but when your child stands next to that clown, she no longer smiles. Despite her deep breaths and efforts to stretch her neck, she's just too short. She doesn't measure up to a standard which, although based on the size of the roller coaster cars, is somewhat arbitrary. It's not a universal or even meaningful standard, yet it has the potential of demoralizing a "too-short" child. She wants to be as tall as that clown's outstretched arm, but the truth is she's as tall as she needs to be right now. Next summer she'll probably be able to ride the Mighty Loop, but even if she isn't, she is—in God's eyes—exactly as tall as she should be.

When we look to Christ as the standard for who we should be and how we should act, we stand face-to-face with the truth of who God calls us to be. We find hope in the fact that God's transforming power is at work in us to conform us to Christ's image (Romans 8:29; 2 Corinthians 3:18). We aren't on our own; we aren't doomed to failure. But when we let another woman become our standard for who we think we should be, we find only frustration.

Keep in mind, however, that comparison is different from imitation. God does give us direction about whom to imitate and the importance of taking this privilege seriously. Scripture clearly tells us to imitate those whose lives are pleasing to the Lord:

> Brethren, join in following my example, and observe those who walk according to the pattern you have in us (Philippians 3:17).

> Be imitators of me, just as I also am of Christ (1 Corinthians 11:1).

> You also became imitators of us and of the Lord, having received the word in much tribulation with the joy of the Holy Spirit (1 Thessalonians 1:6).

For you, brethren, became imitators of the churches of God in Christ Jesus that are in Judea, for you also endured the same sufferings at the hands of your own countrymen, even as they did from the Jews (1 Thessalonians 2:14).

Therefore be imitators of God, as beloved children; and walk in love, just as Christ also loved you (Ephesians 5:1,2).

As Paul lived for Christ . . . so I am to watch what he did and do the same things. When we see God's character displayed in the lives of others, we are to imitate it. We are to "be imitators of God."

Someone's Watching You!

We think of him as a painter, but Renaissance master Leonardo da Vinci was a sculptor, architect, and engineer as well. The artist who created the haunting Mona Lisa actually painted only about 15 pictures, and just three of these were women. *Cecilia Galleran (The Woman in Ermine)* and the wedding portrait *Genevra de Benci* are the other two, and *Genevra* is a very interesting one indeed because, as was a common practice in his day, Da Vinci used both sides of the canvas. On one side, the porcelain-faced beauty captures the viewer's eyes and heart. On the other side are symbols depicting her education, her status in society, and her virtuous character. There is something compelling about the work of art. You can't help but be attracted to this woman. And adding to the intrigue is the conviction of Renaissance scholars that, when this painting was first displayed, you did not see Genevra first. Instead, you saw the symbols that represented her qualities. You noticed first her character and then her appearance.

When I heard this fascinating bit of art history, I started thinking about my own life. What do people see when they look at me? What do I want them to see? What trait would I choose for them to notice most? What really matters?

People do watch us. I first learned this one Sunday morning several years ago. A young wife and mother walked up to me when the worship service was over. Her first words were "You don't know me, but I've been watching you." "Me? What on earth for?" I thought to myself. She continued, "I see how you look so admiringly at your husband during the opening section of our service. And I've noticed your regular attendance, your interest in the sermons, and that big Bible that you carry. Could we have lunch? I'd like to ask you some questions."

During my Sunday afternoon nap later that day, this woman's remarks stirred me. I thought, "What a huge responsibility!" But as I prayed for the young woman and thanked God that I would have a chance to speak of Him to her, I suddenly realized that being with that woman would feel like a job, a "huge responsibility," only if I were concerned about being the kind of person I thought someone *should* watch. But if I continued to try to be the kind of person God wanted me to be, He would use me in her life however He wanted. If I am truly living for Him, being

a Titus 2 older woman is not taking on a different character. It's just being me and letting a younger woman close
enough to see who I am and what's inside.

Keep that perspective in mind as you get used to the
perhaps new idea that, no matter who you are, where you
live, or what you do, someone is probably watching you.
What are they seeing? Are you modeling life as Christ would
have you live it? Are you putting on biblical thinking each
day or are you allowing the culture's way of thinking to guide
your choices and activities? Are you letting God's Word
guide and direct your use of time? Your interactions with
others? Someone is watching you. What are you teaching
her about God and His kingdom?

Are you modeling a godly woman's love for her husband, love for her children, good sense, purity, effective
home management, kindness, and loving subjection to your
husband? Those are lessons that younger women need.

✢ *Mentoring Moment* ✣

Even older women in my life who did not profess Christ of-
ten behaved in godly ways. Mrs. Rubel is one example. The
Rubels owned a small boutique I worked in when I was in high
school. They went out every Saturday night, and made their
time together a priority—something that was unheard of in my
house.

Just as striking as the fact that the Rubels went out every
Saturday was the fact that Mrs. Rubel began getting ready for
her date with her husband—fixing her hair, touching up her
makeup, changing her shoes and often her outfit—an hour or so
before the store closed. It didn't seem necessary to me to "fix up"

to go out with the man you had just spent the day working with, so one day I asked her about her preparations. Her response still echoes in my mind: "Mr. Rubel is the dearest person in the world to me, so I want to look fresh for him across the dinner table."

In so many ways, Mrs. Rubel modeled for me—an impressionable 16-year-old who didn't have any other marriage to watch—how to show a husband how you loved him. I was seeing a love-filled marriage, and I was learning.

Although the Rubels' Jewish heritage was different from my Christian faith, I still learned biblical standards during the three years I worked for them. I also saw beauty, culture, respect, wisdom, and consistency—qualities missing in my own life—in their work, their marriage, and their home. Yes, Mrs. Rubel opened her house to me. She lived out the hospitality that we are to show other people, and she gave me a front-row seat from which to keep watching and keep learning.

Consider the advice Susanna Wesley's father offered her. He said that what counts is not to be "rich in money [or, I would add, knowledge] but rich in character, determination, and intellect." Abraham Lincoln observed, "Character is like a tree and reputation like its shadow. The shadow is what we think of it; the tree, the real thing." Character is real; character is authenticity—and the ability to be authentic has always been an important goal for me. We who are commanded to pass on to younger women important lessons about being the people God wants us to be must be authentic in our modeling, and authenticity comes with living life.

Following the will of God—thinking according to His values, His commands, His purposes, His standards—enables us to pass on to the next generation our love of and knowledge of our Lord and Creator. Thinking God's thoughts enables us to be His beacons, His light, His salt. It also enables us to watch people, see *their* character, and learn from them whatever God would show us. And it enables those who watch us to see God in us and learn what He would have them learn. This is part of God's plan and far removed from destructive comparison.

Comparison Keeps You from Being Uniquely You

"For Thou didst form my inward parts; Thou didst weave me in my mother's womb. I will give thanks to Thee, for I am fearfully and wonderfully made; wonderful are Thy works, and my soul knows it very well." These words of King David in Psalm 139:13,14 are words that you, too, can sing—unless you are too busy looking at other people and imagining how you fall short of being like them.

Comparing yourself to other people prevents you from acknowledging the truth that God made you, that He made only one of you, and that He made you unique. Your gifts, your family heritage, your appearance, your brainpower—these characteristics and many others make you totally unique in all the history of the human race. You are an individual, different from any other person, so why do you want to look like, think like, and act like someone else? Why not enjoy the fact that you are a one-of-a-kind and much-loved creation of your heavenly Father?

We can't enjoy our unique status as God's special child when we insist on scanning the crowd around us to see how we compare. And nothing chips away at our self-confidence like that kind of vigilance. You know how it works. You buy a new dress for a special event. The fabric, the cut, the color, the fit, the price—it's perfect for you and for the occasion. But when you arrive at the party and start looking around and making comparisons, suddenly what was perfect can seem woefully inadequate, can't it? When we do this same sort of comparing of other aspects of ourselves, we find it hard to feel good about being the unique person God has created us to be. Looking to Him rather than at the people around us can help free us to be ourselves and to enjoy our own decisions, choices, and approach to this gift called life.

Comparison Clouds Our Sense of Who We Are

Author Robert Fulghum tells a story about a game called "Giants and Dwarfs" that speaks to what we can lose when we compare ourselves to others. As a group of children gets ready to play the game, the leader counts them off into two groups. One will be the giants; the other the dwarfs. When the leader finishes, a little girl goes up to him and says, "Where do the mermaids go?" He says, "There are no mermaids"—to which she responds, "Yes, there are! I are one!"

This little girl knows who she is. She doesn't let what the people around her are saying and doing weaken her understanding of herself or undermine her acceptance of herself. Former First Lady Barbara Bush is another wonderful real-life example of this. Clearly, even in the media spot-light, she was comfortable with who she is, and she let her faux pearls and stature become her trademark. It would have been all too easy to compare herself to her predeces-sor (rail-thin and solid-gold Nancy Reagan), but then Mrs. Bush would have missed out on the opportunity to be who God has made her and called her to be. She would have missed out on the special mission He has for her alone.

So, like the young mermaid and Mrs. Bush, be your-self. Know that you, in your uniqueness, have a niche—a mission and a ministry—that only you can fill. Revel in that special, God-given role and stand strong in the fact that God made only one of you.

Comparison Undermines God's Leadership in Your Life

God has a plan for your life and mine (Jeremiah 29:11). When we are living out life as ourselves, focused on Him, we can be sensitive to His leadership as that plan un-folds. We will notice the gentle nudge or firm push that keeps us going in the direction He has chosen for us. But when we compare ourselves to other people and try to act like someone we're not, we may easily miss God's plan for our life. When our eyes are fixed too much on other people, we can't pay attention to the Lord who wants to guide our steps and direct our paths.

Consider the example Jesus gives us. He didn't fit in with the religious establishment of His day, and He didn't try to. Instead, He did what God directed. He didn't use the healing methods of His time. Instead, He offered spittle from the ground, the touch of His hand, His spoken word, and the hem of His robe. He was Himself, the unique Son of God, the Person God designed Him to be. True to that design, Jesus could respond when God called, and He could do so in the manner God directed. Jesus was Himself, and that freed Him up to be God's perfect Servant rather than a slave to peers, tradition, people's expectations, or society's ways.

I haven't always known that kind of freedom. I remember, for instance, when the idea of making goals was first introduced to me. I read over a friend's list of goals and thought, "These look great! I'll do the same!" What a frustrating year followed—a year of almost no spiritual or personal growth. Reading the goals of my friend next to me at that goal-setting seminar made her—rather than my heavenly Master and Lord—the leader of my life for that disastrous year.

Beware of Your Own Expectations

We also do ourselves a great disservice when we set unrealistic goals for ourselves and then compare ourselves to that ideal. As we learn to look at Christ's standards for us and to appreciate our own God-given uniqueness, we need to also beware of developing false and unhealthy expectations of ourselves.

To keep from developing such expectations, often we simply need to recognize our limitations. We need to acknowledge the truth about such things as our education, our resources, our family situation, and our physical being. At 5'6", for example, we can't expect a contract with a professional basketball team. If we only speak English, we can't expect an exciting career in international diplomacy. If we have eight children under the age of 16, we can't expect to maintain a home of solitude. We need to adjust our expectations for ourselves according to God's leading as well as to the stage of life we are in, the gifts and talents He has blessed us with, and the ministry to which He has called us.

As you begin sharing your life with another woman of God, consider how much you are still laboring under this burden of not living up to expectations you've had for yourself. What have you expected that has not come to pass? Were those unrealistic expectations? Have you failed to acknowledge that the Sovereign God created you to be exactly who you are and placed you just where He wants you to be?

Resting in God's sovereignty is key to following in the apostle Paul's footsteps and learning to be content in all circumstances (Philippians 4:11). It takes practice to learn to accept God's plan. It isn't easy to die to oneself. But when you and I don't accept God's plan for who we are or where we are or what we are doing, we mock His perfect ways and His perfect love. Comparing ourselves to unrealistic expectations for ourselves as well as to the women around us is wasted energy. Such comparisons will rob you of being all you can be in your service to God, your family, and your friends.

Now say again with David—speak the words aloud and wholeheartedly—"Thou didst form my inward parts; Thou didst weave me in my mother's womb. I will give thanks to Thee, for I am fearfully and wonderfully made; wonderful are Thy works, and my soul knows it very well." Amen!

8

A Unique Way of Giving

As you may have already discovered, you have a unique opportunity to be a Titus 2 woman to your own daughter, and you may also play that special role in the lives of your friends' daughters. These two types of special relationships are to be cherished and handled with great care.

Your Own Daughter

One way to cherish and protect your relationship with your daughter is to evaluate your motives as you develop a relationship with another young woman. If you are seeking a young woman to mentor because your own daughter has left home, hurt you, or disappointed you, you are only inviting further grief in your relationship with her. Daughters of the heart must not be a part of your life so that you can show your own daughter what a wonderful woman you are—and I've seen this happen. One woman I know, though unaware of what she was doing, flaunted her relationship with her younger woman before her biological daughter. When the situation reached fever pitch, the yelling began and the truth came out. Surprised by what she realized about herself, the woman asked her daughter to forgive her, but the pain lasted for a long time.

My point is this: Your own daughter must never be put aside for a daughter of your heart. In my relationship with Kim, whom we talked about earlier, I have always sought our daughter Anissa's counsel in areas where I was unsure. For instance, Kim lives in our town, but our daughter lives in California. It's easy for me to pick up some extras at the market for Kim, and no one minds that. However, when Kim first moved in, it was imperative that I talk to Anissa about which room would be Kim's. Anissa willingly shared her own bedroom with Kim, but that is an arrangement I certainly never would have made without Anissa's input. Then, on another occasion, I had a Christmas gift idea for Kim, but I felt led to ask Anissa what she thought about our giving Kim a certain item from our home. Anissa responded openly and honestly, saying, "Gee, Mom, I'm not sure. I may want that myself someday." And David and I respected her wishes. We would never push our own daughter aside in the least little way and put another woman ahead of her. (At the same time that we are careful with our own daughters—and we need to be—we must also not let them dictate what God would have us do in nurturing a young woman whom God sends our way.)

When you open your life to a younger woman, you need to remember that your natural daughter is in a very different category from any other woman God calls you to reach out to. Your own daughter needs to know that she is not being usurped, replaced, pushed aside, demoted, or slighted. She needs to know that you love her as much as always and that absolutely no other relationship with anyone else will ever change your love for her.

When your own daughter rests secure in your love for her, the rewards for both of you will be immeasurable. I know I will always remember one of the more tangible rewards I received from Anissa a few years ago. A tiny little package came in the mail. The accompanying note read, "Mom, this is for you because you have been to me—and to many others—what this song describes, and you always will be this to me. Now follow the directions." (My daughter knows me! I am one who reads directions only after I have figured it out for myself but have some pieces left over!) Her instructions were: "1. Get a hankie (maybe two). 2. Find a quiet spot. 3. Play this tape to the end." I obeyed completely. I got my handkerchief, went to our bedroom, plugged in the tape recorder, and listened. It was a beautiful song called *The Wind Beneath My Wings*, which spoke of my being a support in my daughter's life, a model as she grew up, and a strength that enabled her to become the woman she is today.

The singer finished, and the next voice was my own dear daughter's saying, "I love you, Mama." It was once again clear to me that Anissa knows her mom well! I needed that handkerchief!

My heart beat wildly and tears of thanksgiving flowed as I realized that my then-19-year-old daughter was acknowledging that I had helped her along the road of life. You and I absolutely never want to jeopardize this precious mother-daughter relationship as we welcome the women whom the Lord sends our way.

Whose Daughter Is She?

Just as we must keep our own daughter aware that she is ours in a very unique and special way and that we will let nothing and no one threaten or alter that relationship, we need to keep in mind that every woman is someone else's daughter in that same special and sacred way. We must always remember to whom she belongs.

All too often a young woman will seek out a strong mother figure because her own mother has not offered her a good model. The parenting she received may not only have been weak but negative and even destructive. Her mother may have hurt her deeply. Abuse can come in a variety of forms, but its wounds always run deep. To help you keep the right perspective on a woman who didn't have godly or healthy parenting, I share with you the rock-solid perspective of my older and very wise friend Mabel.

Mabel and her husband had been married more than 50 years when he died. They raised a family together, worshiped God together, and served Him together. When her dear husband died, Mabel decided to invest herself and some of her time in young women—and she has been amazing in this role. Every young woman who enters her life is richly blessed by Mabel's complete and unabashed love for Christ.

In a talk Mabel once gave, she told about a tragedy in her life. She spoke gently with her lovely Canadian accent: "Stan and I lived in a rural area, and our children were born at home. When our second son was born, the doctor came just as we needed him. The delivery was hard, but not too bad. We heard our son cry, and then suddenly—within ten minutes or so—he was dead. Later we learned that the doctor was drunk and, as a result, killed our baby."

People in the room fell silent. Then some women spoke up softly, saying things that would only be asked in the nineties—"Did you sue?" "I hope he lost his license!" "He should never have delivered another baby!"

Mabel listened to their words and then spoke these simple but profound words: "My God could have saved my baby."

She wasn't bitter or vengeful. She knew her God and His love and power. The measure of her faith and trust in God touched all of us to the very core of our being. When tragedy strikes, how easy it is for us to forget that our omniscient, omnipresent, omnipotent God reigned even as it occurred and that He still reigns. When we come close to another's pain (or even when we're overwhelmed by our own), we can forget He is the Redeemer God, the Romans 8:28 God, the God who shares our sorrows and our hurts.

But Mabel didn't forget who God is, and Mabel's God is the same God who allowed that special but hurting woman whom He sent your way to be raised by her mother and father, whatever pain she experienced in that relationship. As you share with a woman who has been wounded by her parents, always remember that her loving Creator has plans for her that are good (Jeremiah 29:11) and that you are in the privileged place of being used by Him, of being an instrument in His hands, as He accomplishes His good.

Then, mindful of the fact that this woman of God is another person's daughter, model Mabel's lack of bitterness and vengefulness. Encourage this sister in the Lord who has been deeply hurt to share openly and honestly her feelings about her lack of parenting. Help her to learn new lessons to replace the wrong ones she was taught and to learn what she never learned as a child. But don't speak against her mother, and never try to take her mother's place. (That advice holds true for any and every mentoring situation, whatever kind of parenting the other woman received.)

Each step of the way, whatever your friend's story, you are to be a model and an encourager, but not a mother. Many of the tasks you perform in the relationship with a younger woman look and feel very much like mothering, but they are *not*. Your primary goal is to point her in the direction of the Savior. In the case of a woman wounded by her natural mother, your additional goal is to help her establish a relationship with her own mother (Romans 12:18).

So, as you set forth God's standards for parenting and as you model His plan for motherhood, help your hurting sister identify positive qualities about her mother. Encourage her to affirm her mother in those areas where her mother succeeded. Do what you can to lead her to a place of reconciliation and peace with her mother. Offer her comfort in her pain but continue to point her in the direction of forgiveness. Indeed, you might have been a "better" mother to her, but you were not the one God chose. He did choose you to be her Titus 2 woman, and that is truly a great honor. What a privilege to be a beacon of God's truth and light, His forgiveness and healing, and to help her find her worth and discover hope in the unconditional and redemptive love of her Creator God and learn how to live a life of holiness that glorifies Him.

Your Friends' Daughters

About five years ago I was doing a live call-in radio show when a woman phoned, asked several questions, and then, departing from her topic, said, "Donna, if you could give a mother another name, what would it be?" I said a quick prayer for wisdom and, in thirty seconds or so, responded with "facilitator." After all, as mothers we assist our children by giving them a full and rich life experience. We teach them, train them, and, as old Auntie Mame would say, "open new windows" in their lives.

As a mother, I've wanted Anissa to have the rich blessing of knowing my friends and peers. So I encouraged her relationships with those women, and almost all of them were delighted to be a part of my daughter's life—and I was delighted to have them! For instance, since my friend Joan and Anissa have the same temperament, they have loads in common and both especially enjoy poking fun at yours truly! My friend Martha (Anissa called her "Mrs. Martha") did all the domestic things Anissa could never learn from me. My friend Ann happened to be the mother of one of Anissa's high-school chums, and her home was Anissa's home-away-from-home. "Aunt" Mary, who is as different from me as night is from day, nevertheless has the very same belief system and often gave Anissa advice that I whole-heartedly agreed with. In fact, because of this special relationship, Anissa attended Aunt Mary's college alma mater. When Anissa was 15, another friend of mine, who was associated with the missions organization Overseas Crusade, put us in touch with a family who invited Anissa to spend the summer in France helping missionary families. Anissa cleaned, cooked, baked, cared for the children, assisted in the office, and did any other work she was able to do. Each of these wonderful, unique women—first my friends and then every one a Titus 2 woman for my dear Anissa—brought a dimension into her life that David and I could not. Among other things, they taught her to be accepting of and open to a variety of people. I never felt threatened by their relationships with our daughter. These women were and are my friends. I trusted them with my daughter, and I trusted them to remember the differences between my role in her life and theirs. They invested their lives into hers and consequently find some reward in Anissa's accomplishments.

Such consciousness of the fact that the young woman you are coming alongside is your friend's daughter is crucial when it comes to figuring out how close to draw near. This particular type of relationship is definitely a bit trickier than others God sends our way! Consider that you've probably known this young woman from times when her family and yours got together. This kind of history makes your relationship unique. Then, moving from being a friend to her mother to also being a Titus 2 woman to her means adding a new dimension to both relationships. Now you are a channel of God's love and guidance to the younger woman in a more personal way.

But being an older woman to this younger woman is often a logical and quite natural relationship. After all, if your style of friendship is like mine or if you were trained by a mother like me, you seldom just take a friend into your life. You also get to know (or at least know about) her husband. You know her grandchildren, her other friends, her parents, her siblings, her heritage—you know her world. Furthermore, the trust that you've established with your friend makes it easier for her to let you get close to her daughter, and that new dimension to the relationsip can help your friend as well as her daughter.

I remember Anissa's early years of college when she was redefining her thoughts about men, dating, and marriage and thinking through issues about her appearance. During a meeting with my Chaber group (*chaber* means "bound together" in Hebrew), one of my friends offered to discuss these issues with Anissa over breakfast. During the meal, Naomi shared with Anissa a box shaped like a Bible. Inside it, she had some notes—answers from God's Word—for Anissa to keep. After pointing Anissa to God's Word, Naomi offered her opinions and ideas. Much of what she said Anissa already knew, but hearing it from someone other than dear ol' Mom gave the words of truth new power and significance. I am so thankful for Naomi and her willingness to give her ideas to Anissa.

My generation was eager to take on this kind of responsibility for one another's children. As young mothers, we regularly cared for and even taught our friends' children. When Anissa was little, for example, she and I spent hours with my friend Jan and her son Jeff, who is one year older than Anissa. The little ones played, ate, bathed, and napped together. Being part of such a foursome, I found it easy and natural to say, "No, Jeff. You can't have any more candy." And it was just as easy for Jan to change Anissa's diaper or remind her about the importance of sharing.

Even today, I still stop a child on the street who is damaging property and tell him I am headed for his parents' home to report him. (Old habits die hard!) I believe that children grow to respect adults when we exercise authority in this manner. And I believe that we parents do well to let adults we trust help us raise our children by giving those adults the freedom to exercise authority over our kids and offer godly advice that is consistent with what we have taught them.

During Anissa's college years, she sought advice on a certain matter from one of my friends, and that friend told me of the call before Anissa did. When I later asked Anissa why she hadn't called us, her explanation made perfect sense. She said, "Mom, I know what you and Dad think about this issue. I wanted another opinion—the opinion of someone you and Dad trust." Thinking of her words still brings tears of joy to my eyes and makes me thankful for my friend's presence in Anissa's life as well as my own.

The daughter of a friend may seek you out as Anissa did in this situation. She may want just a single bit of advice, or she may find herself at a shaky point in her life and in need of the additional support of her parents' friends. Whatever the circumstances, the following guidelines will help when your friends' daughters turn to you:

~ Let your friend know about your prayerful decision to come alongside her daughter in a Titus 2 way. In some situations, it may be wise to seek your friend's permission before you add this new dimension to your relationship with her daughter.

~ Remain loyal to your friend and make sure her daughter knows you will remain a loyal friend to her mother.

~ Stay close to your friend during the time you meet with her daughter. Don't give the enemy cause to attack her by preying on any jealous feelings or any sense of rivalry.

~ Never blame your friend for whatever circumstances have caused her daughter to turn to you. The situation may or may not be her fault (there are two sides to every story!), but that is God's business. While it is okay and even important for the young woman to share her feelings, never let her speak ill about her mother. Also, demonstrate understanding without allowing disrespect or disobedience.

∾ Support your friend through your older woman/ younger woman relationship with her daughter, especially if there has been a breach in their relationship.

Throughout your relationship with your friend's daughter, remember that if God has ordained this relationship, you are ultimately helping your friend in her parenting role at the same time that you are helping her daughter. This bond of love for her daughter can deepen your relationship with your friend, and all three of you will benefit. One more thing. As with any Titus 2 relationship, know that fruit is often seen later. Progress may be slow, but be patient. You are doing God's work and He will bless.

Even with the above guidelines, being an older woman to a friend's daughter can be, as I've said, tricky business. I have had failure as well as success in this area, and the failure was very painful. My friend and her daughter were at odds, and encouraging this daughter to be reconciled to her mother was one of my main topics whenever we met. One day, however, the mother approached me and said, "If you weren't in my daughter's life, I feel certain I would be!" Ouch! No one will ever know how those words crushed me. But they also forced me to evaluate my relationship with my friend and with her daughter and to realize that I had broken one of my own rules. I had not stayed close to my friend while I was drawing closer to her daughter.

On a more positive note, I have had the enormous joy of watching a daughter of a friend—a daughter of my heart—become a woman more in love with the Lord. What a privilege! Few experiences match the exhilaration I felt when this young woman came to me and said, "Donna, I need another woman to learn from." There are no problems at all between this woman and her mother. This young woman just needed a different voice at that time, and her mother let me in because she had her daughter's best interest at heart. In fact, my friend said that nothing made her happier than knowing I was praying for her daughter and being a channel of God's love, truth, and guidance. (In fact, it was this friend who helped me formulate the guidelines I shared above for being an older woman to a friend's daughter.)

Let me share another story about drawing close to a friend's daughter. When Martha walked into my heart, she brought her daughters with her. We laughed and played together. They drove my car, wore my clothes, and cared for Anissa. When Martha's daughter Lisa called to tell me she had become officially engaged, we talked about the wedding and she spoke of the place I had in her heart. (As plans for the wedding developed, David and I learned we would be privileged to serve as host and hostess at Lisa and Billy's wedding reception.) Although Lisa—like each of her sisters—is very close to her mother, I have been blessed to play a part in this family that loves and serves God. I have had the opportunity to praise God's works and declare His mighty acts to Martha's daughters (Psalm 145:4). Martha's girls want my counsel, my ideas, and my help. What a joy and what an honor!

God's Blessed Ways

My mother was angry one day because I wouldn't do what she wanted me to do. Although this scene happened many years ago, I still remember her saying, "If your Aunt Pat asked you to clean the toilet, you'd say, 'How many times?'" Over the years, I've thought about her words. She was probably right, and I don't really understand why the dynamics between mother and daughter are so different from the dynamics between a woman who is her mother's peer and that daughter. I surrender that, with countless other things, to the Isaiah 55:8 category of life ("My thoughts are not your thoughts, neither are your ways My ways. . . . For as the heavens are higher than the earth, so are My ways higher than your ways, and My thoughts than your thoughts"). I don't have any explanation. I just know that our Lord powerfully uses godly older women in the lives of younger women to show them His ways, His truth, and His standards for this life. It was He who ordained and commanded that older women train younger women in the areas of godliness, marriage, mothering, and homemaking. And, as I'm sure you know by now, I feel it's one of the most blessed relationships to be involved in whether you're giving or receiving!

Remember the song Anissa had me listen to? Here are a few lines:

Did you ever know that you're my hero,
You're everything I would like to be?

I can fly higher than an eagle.
You are the wind beneath my wings.

—Larry Henley and Jeff Silbar

What did I do to deserve the gift of these words? What made her believe that I, her mother, was the "wind beneath [her] wings" and, as a friend to others, the "wind beneath [their] wings"? The only answer I have is that, like King David, I have discovered that "under [God's] wings [we] may seek refuge; His faithfulness is a shield and bulwark" (Psalm 91:4). I believe that since I had sought God and found Him and experienced His protective faithfulness, He could then use me as a refuge and source of comfort, instruction, and support for others, including my own daughter.

You, my fellow older women, have undoubtedly found God to be your refuge, your shield, your bulwark. If you share that truth with a younger sister in the Lord, you will have done great things toward passing on to the next generation the truth of God and an example of how to live a life that pleases Him.

Thank You, Lord, for Your wisdom, Your grace, and this special and wonderful calling to pass on Your kingdom to the next generation.

9

Frustrations and Farewells

In 1994 I met a 23-year-old woman from Romania. The mother of three small children, she and her dear husband had opened their home as a residential care facility for the elderly—as his parents had done and their parents before them.

In November of 1994, this young woman's six-month-old baby died in a tragic accident. Her mother, her husband's mother, her sisters, and her friends were there with her, and they helped her through this time of pain and grief. But in a conversation just weeks after the funeral, she thanked me for the message of hope I was able to bring. As an older woman in her life—not a family member or a peer—I occupy a unique place in her life. God used me to meet a need that another young friend and even her own mother could not meet. And He can use you in the very same way to give to another of His daughters exactly what she needs.

Each of us, however, will give differently because each of us is one of God's unique creations and because each woman He brings into our life for this special Titus 2 relationship is also a precious, one-of-a-kind creation of the King. Some relationships will be challenging, as we will discuss in this chapter. Some relationships will last only a short season. Some will become friendships for life. Given the uniqueness of us human beings, our personal style of friendships, and our distinct personalities, relationships with one another can vary widely.

A Woman Who Refines Us

"Oh, no. Here she comes again. If only she weren't such an incessant chatterbox, forever asking questions that have already been answered. . . . If only she would listen. . . . *Lord, perhaps You could send a distraction and change her path. No, here she comes.*"

You probably wouldn't expect thoughts like these to run through the mind of a woman of God as the woman God has brought into her life approaches. But thoughts like these do in fact come when we are sent a woman we may not want—specifically, a woman God sends to refine us. And I hope my honesty doesn't offend, but I speak of this kind of relationship because I have been a difficult daughter of the heart and because God has sent such a daughter of the heart to me.

Let me share about the time I was a difficult daughter of the heart. I remember, for instance, times when I knew all too clearly what I should do in a given situation. God had made it clear to me, but I didn't want to take action. (It's so much easier just to talk forever and forever about the issues rather than to act on them, isn't it?) I know now that I called this dear woman too often and tried to find an easy way around her very direct responses to my questions. I am certain by the tone of her voice and her husband's that, although I know they loved me, there were times they wished I would just go away. In circumstances like these, it's important to determine if the pursuing and/or irritating woman is being sent to you by God. If so, what are you to do with her?

First, keep in mind that in some cases a woman of God is sought after because she has power, influence, wealth, education, heritage, fame, notoriety, a contagious sense of fun, a famous husband, a husband who is a pastor, or because her ministry to other women has been so positive that many others want to be close to her. A woman who is sought after for any of these reasons—and you may be in such a position—needs to realize that she cannot possibly make time for every woman who writes or calls her. Only God can direct you to the woman in whom He would have you invest time and energy. You must know His voice and then be obedient to what He instructs. And, actually, such confidence that the Lord is bringing a particular woman into your life so that you can pass on your knowledge of and love for Him is key to any Titus 2 relationship between women of God. His direction, His guidance, and His voice—this is how we know if a woman (difficult or delightful) is the one with whom God would have us share our life.

Now on to the second point. If God is clearly sending this difficult woman into your life, how are you to handle her?

First, remember that God's plan for us is always best and that the methods He uses to refine us are His business, not ours. When the Lord first gave me a difficult daughter of the heart, I realized that she was there to teach me. But would I be teachable? Would I let myself be taught, refined, sharpened by this woman God had sent to me? The decision to receive this gift from my heavenly Father was mine alone.

I did receive this young woman, and that's when the Lord changed my exasperation with her. He did so by opening my eyes to my own behavior toward one of the older women earlier in my life. God forced me to acknowledge my insensitivity to family times in her home and the occasions when I had taken too many liberties. He showed me how I had usurped her time and disregarded her boundaries. This look back at my life forced me to answer God's question to me about the difficult daughter of the heart He was sending me—"Donna, what were you like at her age?"—and then to accept her and extend to her His love and compassion.

When God sends a difficult, troublesome, or irritating woman your way, He also provides the love and grace you need to be able to be a beacon of His light to her. Keep in mind that you receive God's grace and His love for this difficult woman when you pray. In fact, "Pray" is the best one-word answer to the question, "What do I do with this troublesome or irritating person?" Pray for her—and pray for yourself and the lessons God would have you learn from her. (As you see God answer this ongoing prayer, you will realize that God often uses such a woman in your life more than He uses you in hers!)

And what are some of the lessons, by God's grace, a difficult daughter of the heart will help teach you? Well, she will teach you the importance of relying on the Lord by keeping you on your knees and humble before Him. She will also teach you to set and maintain boundaries (but know going into this that a difficult daughter of your heart will test every boundary you set!).

In *Ordering Your Private World,* Gordon MacDonald tells about being in his study one Saturday, the day he set aside for final sermon preparation. When the phone rang, he answered it. The woman on the other end was clearly upset and said, "I must see you now! It's urgent." Being young, he stopped his final sermon preparation and went to the church to meet her. When he got there he discovered that this difficulty had been going on for many years.[5]

The next time he got a call like this, he immediately asked how long the caller had been dealing with the situation. After learning that it was not an emergency, Pastor MacDonald explained that he would be preaching three times the next day, was occupied with his sermon, and would be unable to give the caller his total attention. He then said, "Since this has been going on for several years, it can wait until Monday. Call me in the morning and we'll set up an appointment." He had realized that he would be the one to blame if he let others rob him of his time—and the same is true for you and me. Remember that there is time enough to do all that God wants us to do.

5. Gordon MacDonald, *Ordering Your Private World* (Nashville: Oliver Nelson, a division of Thomas Nelson, Inc., Publishers, 1984, 1985), pp. 77-78.

So what will you do if this difficult woman calls at dinnertime? Be firm and tell her you will have time for her tomorrow. If she asks for 10 minutes and you're certain she'll take 20, respond with, "You know how easy it is to talk longer than 10 minutes! I'll set my timer to help us stay on track." Such responses are not rejection. They are a way of training a difficult daughter of the heart and helping her learn lessons for life at the same time that you use your time wisely.

A Faltering Daughter of the Heart

A young woman who wants help but is so weak she hardly knows where to begin offers different relational challenges. This woman knows that she needs you, you hear God calling you to be there for her, and so the two of you start meeting together. But it's not long until you are completely frustrated. This woman's life skills are so poor and her experience in right living so minimal that, no matter what happens in life and no matter how you coach her, she seems to fall off the log.

Delores was just such a woman. When she first came to our Mentors for Moms program, her hair was often dirty, matted, and uncombed. She always wore dark clothes (to hide the dirt?), and her shoes were never polished. Most distressing was her cynical attitude toward life and her skepticism about whether the Bible's values, standards, and guidelines could work in real life. Could a godly woman who lived according to the Lord's Word really make it? "After all," she often said, "this is the nineties!" And this woman, you say, was in Mentors for Moms? Yes, because we only have two requirements: The moms have to want to come and demonstrate that by faithfully attending, and the mentors have to love Jesus. Delores met the requirement: Her surprisingly (to us) faithful attendance clearly showed us that she really wanted to come.

Problems arose early for Delores and her mentor. First, Delores desired far greater change than she was able to accomplish. She desperately wanted to change. She saw young women eager for God; she wasn't. She saw good marriages; hers was in a shambles. She heard about neat homes; hers was a disaster. Despite these grand goals, her mentor saw very little progress at all. Furthermore, Delores poked fun at her mentor's "corny" ideas about family life. Her skepticism seemed to make her deaf to anything her mentor said. Still, the mentor stayed faithful, listening and offering assistance whenever she could, praying for and loving this young woman whom she knew God had sent.

Well, at the end of the Mentors for Moms year, dear Delores rose to her feet. Her hair was clean and combed, and she wore a bright floral dress, pearls at her neck, and a new pair of beige shoes on her feet. Tears fell like rain from my eyes as I listened to her explain what the past 12 months had done for her. (Her physical appearance told all of us a great deal even before she opened her mouth!) First, Delores affirmed the steadfastness of her mentor. She also explained that the word *friend* was not one she threw around easily, but she could most certainly say that her mentor had become her friend. Then Delores ended by saying, "I realize I haven't accomplished in these 12 months all I hoped to—and certainly not as much as my mentor had hoped I would. But I will take with me, for the rest of my life, the godly attributes I saw her live out." She was changed in the presence of a holy God.

So don't despair over a faltering young woman. Walk with her and let her grow at her speed. After all, we must have different standards for each person, and your standards for someone who is faltering need to fit her. Say what you feel God wants you to say. Sow the seed of His truth and His Word. Do what you can to nurture that seed, but trust the harvest to Him. Also, trust this faltering sister to Him. Trust that God is at work in her heart despite what you are seeing or not seeing. He doesn't give up on any of us, so don't give up on her.

Relationships for a Season

"Messenger of Sympathy and Love, Servant of Parted Friends . . ."—these words are part of the motto etched above the portals of the U.S. Post Office in Washington, D.C. And these words are especially meaningful when we consider women of God who are with us only for a season.

It's a bittersweet fact that women we draw close to may not stay in our life forever. So cherish the time you have with them. At the same time, don't cling or let their growth or dependency on you become your sole source of affirmation. (That's God's role!) Following these two guidelines will make letting go easier when the time comes. You—and she—will probably still shed some tears, but among the tears of sadness at parting will be tears of joy for what you two have been able to share.

I know about tears when it comes to saying good-bye, for I had to say good-bye to Wendy. When I met Wendy in a Bible-study class I was teaching in my church, I saw right away that we were kindred spirits. We struck up an instant friendship that, rooted in Christ's love, quickly deep-ened.

Wise for her years and eager to be all she could be in Christ, Wendy sought my advice in the very areas God calls us older women to give advice in. She was quick to challenge me, and I was just as quick to make certain my information was accurate. She also helped me understand more about the pressures an educated older mother feels and how she makes her decisions. She taught me much during our time together.

After a few years, she and her husband decided to go to the mission field for two years, and that step seemed perfect for their family. I felt sad when they left, but Wendy's letters were frequent. She also visited and called when they were in the States on furlough.

At the end of their two years of missions work, Wendy's family headed home to a house that we knew had been poorly maintained by the tenants. With the help of many of their friends and a few of mine, their home was transformed by new carpeting, new curtains, new furniture, and new paint from top to bottom. When the family arrived home, their own books were in the bookcase and their family photos on the table.

"Welcome back, daughter of my heart!" I thought. But within six months her husband decided to move his family to another state and change careers. This time I faced letting go permanently—except through the mail.

Standing True to God's Call

Like any work we do, ministering as a Titus 2 woman will have its frustrations as well as its joys, its happy moments as well as its sad ones. When God sends us a woman to help refine us and make us more Christlike, the Titus 2 ministry can be especially challenging. When He sends a faltering daughter our way, the ministry can be discouraging. And when He shows us that it's time to say good-bye to one we've come to love, our ministry can become quite bittersweet.

Therefore, throughout our Titus 2 relationships—and they'll be as rich and varied as God's daughters themselves are—we do well to make the words of the following hymn our heartfelt commitment and prayer.

I Would Be True

I would be true, for there are those who trust me;
I would be pure, for there are those who care;
I would be strong, for there is much to suffer;

I would be brave, for there is much to dare,
I would be brave, for there is much to dare.

I would be friend of all, the foe, the friendless;
I would be giving, and forget the gift;
I would be humble, for I know my weakness;
I would look up and laugh and love and lift,
I would look up and laugh and love and lift.

—Howard Arnold Walter

Our heavenly Father will indeed honor such a woman of God who says, "Here am I! Use me in the life of the precious child You send my way" and then keeps her eyes on Him as she serves. Always remember that difficult, faltering, or distant, the joy of being involved with a fellow sojourner is enormous.

10

Rave Reviews

When I was a child, one of my favorite pastimes was reading. I had an especially hard time putting down the biographies and autobiographies I opened. Perhaps even as a child I enjoyed watching through the pages of a book how someone else lived and learning why they did what they did. Although these men and women were leaps and bounds ahead of me in character and faith, I knew that in some ways each of them was just like me, and this realization stimulated me to good deeds.

During the late eighties, I had the opportunity to hear author and speaker Jean Lush. As I listened to this delightful woman, her elderly face framed by beautiful white hair, I was amazed by the frankness with which this woman—at least 30 years my senior—spoke. It was absolutely exhilarating. Thirty minutes into her message, it hit me. When you get old or older, you can say a lot more than you were able to say when you were young. I'd found yet another reason to celebrate growing older.

A few months later I talked to Elisabeth about my observation. "Is it true that as you get older you are able to say more than you did when you were young?" I asked. Elisabeth, who is nearly 20 years older than me, stated in true Elisabeth style, "Certainly," and promptly sent me the following piece:

Prayer for the Middle-Aged
By a 17th-Century Nun

Lord, Thou knowest better than I know myself
that I am growing old.
Keep me from the fatal habit of thinking
I must say something on every subject
and on every occasion.
Release me from craving to straighten out everybody's affairs.
Make me thoughtful but not moody, helpful but not bossy.
With my vast store of wisdom it seems a pity
not to use it all, but Thou knowest, Lord,
that I want a few friends at the end.
Keep my mind free from the recital of endless details;
give me wings to get to the point.
Seal my lips on my aches and pains.
They are increasing, and love of rehearsing them is
becoming sweeter as the years go by.
I dare not ask for grace enough to enjoy the tales of others' pains,
but help me to endure them with patience.
I dare not ask for improved memory, but
for a growing humility and a lessening cocksureness when
my memory seems to clash with the memories of others.
Teach me the glorious lesson that occasionally I may be mistaken.
Keep me reasonably sweet.
I do not want to be a saint—
some of them are so hard to live with—

but a sour old person is one of the crowning works of the devil.
Give me the ability to see good things in unexpected places
and talents in unexpected people.
Give me the grace to tell them so.
Amen.

I, too, say "Amen" to that prayer! Don't you?

Letters of Today

Like our prayers, our letters can reveal much about us. That's why I want to share with you some letters from older women who have shared themselves and their faith with other (usually younger) women of God. Having talked to these women, I know how timid they were about reaching out. But before they took their first step, I also knew they would be blessed if they did so—yet not even I expected the blessings to be so great.

I wanted to help somewhere in the church. The young woman I received was brand-new in her walk. I could answer every one of her questions with assurance. It made me realize just how much I knew about God and His Word.

After meeting my daughter of the heart, I wondered what God had in mind. I knew she was young and I was old, but I also saw her strengths and her love for God and family. I could not find any holes in her armor, so to speak. It took only about six weeks until I realized that God had sent me to pray for her and with her.

She regularly remarked, "I have learned so much about praying."

I have often struggled with, "What can I, at 70, offer anyone?" I now know. This passage in Titus talks about what I know best—being a Christian, a wife (I've been one for 52 years), a mother, and sharing my home with others. I have time in my world for more than one young woman, and I am going to do this kind of work until I die.

This dear woman died two years after she wrote this letter. When I spoke with her in the hospital, she was so pleased with God's leading in her life. I shall never forget her comment: "I went to help her, and she helped me much more." And listen to this letter:

> ### The Teacher
>
> *Lord, who am I to teach the way*
> *To little children day by day*
> *So prone myself to go astray?*
> *I teach them knowledge, but I*
> *   know*
> *How faint the flicker and how low*
> *The candles of my knowledge glow.*
> *I teach them power to will and do,*
> *But only now I learn anew*
> *My own great weakness through*
> *   and through*
> *I teach them love for all mankind*
> *And all God's creatures, but I find*
> *My love comes lagging far behind.*
> *Lord, if their guide I still must be,*
> *Oh, let the little children see*
> *The teacher leaning hard on Thee.*
>
> —Leslie Pinckney Hill

I figured after 46 years of marriage I had all the answers. However, as the young woman in my life asked me questions about marriage, submission, intimacy, and building her husband up, I came face-to-face with the fact that I needed to do some learning, too. So we learned together, we prayed together, and we saw some changes together. It was very sweet.

Words from the Younger Women

What younger women have said may also help give you a more up-close-and-personal understanding of what a Titus 2 ministry is all about and what it can mean to the women God puts in your life.

How grateful I am that I followed the persistent prompting to get involved in the life of an older woman. How very, very faithful is the Father for He knew my need to be in her presence, to be nourished by her deep well of wisdom, spiritually and experientially. She has encouraged me to fix my eyes on what is eternal and what is a lasting treasure—Jesus.

When I first met my older woman, I was expecting my third child. Daily I felt exhausted and overwhelmed. Then my mentor arrived with love, knowledge, and encouragement. I wanted so desperately to know some practical and biblical applications to being a wife, a mother, a housekeeper, a cook—all the things I was doing at home but without godly insight. She truly set me on the track to being a Proverbs 31 woman. I will never ever be able to thank her for everything she gave me.

The voice of an experienced, godly woman saying what I already believed in my heart to be true about the value of being a keeper of my home, a lover of my husband, and the primary caregiver of my children validated my convictions. I am eternally grateful for her life-changing influence, and I hope to pass that same influence on to the next generation.

(Rereading this letter makes me want to jump up and down! Hooray for her and for her Titus 2 woman!)

You bring to mind heart and home. Your enjoyment of cooking for your family inspires the thought of the kitchen and hearth being the center of the home. The Proverbs 31 woman also provided for her family. She also had a husband who trusted in her, and I have seen this trust between Dick and you. Thank you for being an example to me in these most important areas of family life.

A Chance to Learn

Are all Titus 2 relationships talked about so glowingly? To be honest, I do on very rare occasions hear about a negative experience. When I do, I find those letters important teachers for those of us who respond to God's Titus 2 commands. As an example, let me share some comments from one such letter: "I was so disappointed in my older woman. She was tardy, did not keep her word, and finally admitted she did not have time for me."

A year after I received that letter, I heard from the writer again: "I have given much thought to my frank note of last year. One year later I realize that, although my dream of what a relationship with an older woman would be (I do have a woman in my life now) was dashed, the disappointment taught me a very valuable lesson. I don't want to be old and late in appointments or not able to prioritize my time. I am grateful for what I saw. It taught me what I did not want to be."

God used even this disappointing relationship with an older woman of God to teach the younger woman who watched her some valuable lessons. And of course He uses the rewarding older woman/younger woman relationships to benefit those involved—and their family members as well. Let me close with this delightful example. When a young woman was perplexed about how to handle a given situation in the home, her husband told her, "Call your mentor!" The older woman's positive influence on his wife had so impressed him that he suggested calling her before calling his folks or his wife's!

I hope these letters and stories inspire you because I realize that the charge of Titus 2 can seem overwhelming. Upon reading Paul's words, you may feel that there's only a dim chance that you could ever fulfill the ministry he describes. But as these letters show, you *can* and, with God's blessing, *will* be used by Him to encourage other women in their efforts to be a woman whose life honors Him. In fact, the younger women He calls you to mentor may be feeling there's only a dim chance they can manage all that life entails, but you—by your very presence and due to the fact that you've lived through many of the challenges they now face—will offer them the bright hope that they can and will survive. It's a vital ministry, and it's one that God will enable you to do and do well. Take the step of faith and see!

11

The Fingerprint of God

As we've seen throughout this book, women who model their lives on Titus 2:3-5 become *messengers of God's love* to the next generation and often to their own peers. And, through the years, I've seen that these older women share certain other common characteristics—evidence of God's fingerprints on their lives. A review of the following traits will serve as a reminder that ministry happens between women of God not because older women have crossed some spiritual finish line, but because they are being touched by the Lord's transforming power day by day.

A Heart for God

First and foremost, a woman who has walked with the Lord through the years knows to look for God in all people and all circumstances and knows how to see Him when she looks. This godly woman allows God to truly rule her days, her hours, her minutes. She practices His presence, rests in His lordship, and abides in His love. This kind of heart for God is granted to all who seek Him, and this kind of heart for God makes an older woman a gracious channel of His love for those of us blessed by her presence in our life.

A Teachable Spirit

One of my favorite people in Scripture is Apollos, and you might not even be acquainted with him. We don't hear a lot about him or his work. Most often he is just referred to when members of the early Christian community are asked, "Are you of Apollos or Paul?" Apollos takes center stage, however, in a brief passage in the book of Acts:

> Now a certain Jew named Apollos, an Alexandrian by birth, an eloquent man, came to Ephesus; and he was mighty in the Scriptures. This man had been instructed in the way of the Lord; and being fervent in spirit, he was speaking and teaching accurately the things concerning Jesus, being acquainted only with the baptism of John; and he began to speak out boldly in the synagogue. But when Priscilla and Aquila heard him, they took him aside and explained to him the way of God more accurately.
>
> And when he wanted to go across to Achaia, the brethren encouraged him and wrote to the disciples to welcome him; and when he had arrived, he helped greatly those who had believed through grace; for he powerfully refuted the Jews in public, demonstrating by the Scriptures that Jesus was the Christ (18:24-28).

Notice how this man Apollos is described. He's eloquent, "mighty in the Scriptures," "fervent in spirit," and able to speak and teach accurately. We would do well to have any one of those traits, much less all of them! But the little word that points out Apollos's most desirable trait is the word more at the end of verse 26.

Here's the situation: Priscilla and Aquila come to town and hear Apollos teach. After he is finished, they go up to him and say, "You need to present God's Word more accurately than you already are." Despite his strong credentials and proven effectiveness, Apollos hears what they say and, evidenced by the fact that his ministry continued with the strong support of his fellow believers, apparently agrees and learns and changes. Apollos is teachable. That is the trait I most admire about him—and the one I most want for myself!

Older women who are becoming God's messengers to the next generation know their message on the Lord's behalf, but they also know that the Lord isn't finished with them yet. They know that He will continue to teach them until they go home to be with Him. They are teachable and willing to learn from people of all ages.

Martha was one of God's messengers in my life who was indeed teachable. She was also the answer to a prayer I prayed as I moved back to Chicago. My experiences with older women had been rich up to that point, and now at the age of 27 I expected this pattern to continue. In fact, in my prayers I offered God a list of desirable qualities in the older women He had for me there. I specified that these older women should be intelligent, educated, married, orderly, the manager of an efficient and effective home, interested in art, history, and music, the mother of well-behaved children, and active in their church and community life. I was so arrogant. As if I knew what I needed to make me more a woman after God's own heart!

In response to my prayers, God wisely sent me Martha. Now she had many of the qualities I was looking for, but some important (in my mind) traits were missing. When I went to Martha's home, for instance, we had to move the pile of clean clothes waiting to be folded before we could sit on the sofa for a visit ("the manager of an efficient and effective home"?). Born and raised in the hills of Arkansas, Martha had a high school education ("educated"?). Her interest in art was marginal, and with five daughters she had little time for community activity.

But of course God knew exactly what He was doing when He placed her in my life. Daily, Martha lived out her love for God: She was a friend to many, she spoke forth her beliefs whenever she had an opportunity, and she befriended women, young and old alike. Above all, though, Martha was teachable. She taught me many things as I watched her, and I clearly saw that she was always learning something new. I also realized that I wanted that trait in my life. I was changed forever because Martha allowed herself to be a messenger of the Lord. When I thank God for Martha and think back on how lost I was when He brought her into my life (my home life was in disarray, to put it mildly), I have to quote a song: "I'm forever grateful to You, I'm forever grateful to the Cross/I'm forever grateful to You that You came to seek and save the lost." I was lost when Martha, acting as God's messenger, swooped me up in her arms and offered me everyday lessons on each of the Titus 2 concepts. I am forever grateful she did so.

The Lord's Perspective of Time

While many people live primarily in the past, present, or future, a messenger for God understands that we are never to dwell too long in any one of those time zones. Looking too much at the past can cause us to get stuck on the pain or wax nostalgic for the "good ol' days." Thinking only of the present can look a lot like eating, drinking, and being merry and then having nothing of eternal value to show for our life when it comes to an end. And looking only to the future can lead us to miss the gift of the present as we plan for a tomorrow that may never come. Understanding time and the interconnection of past, present, and future causes us to remember God's faithfulness in the past, enjoy His gift of the present, anticipate His redemptive coming again, and celebrate the truth that "Jesus Christ is the same yesterday and today, yes and forever" (Hebrews 13:8). What a testimony such an understanding is!

Having our heavenly Father's perspective on time also means realizing that we are to invest in the next generation of His people. With this heaven-bound rather than earth-bound mind-set, God's messengers are aware that everything they do and say affects future generations (statistics tell us for four generations!).

A Willingness to Share Their Knowledge of God

Jesus' great commission to share the good news of God's forgiving love and to make disciples of all nations (Matthew 28:19) is a command to you and me, not a special assignment strictly for trained public speakers, Bible teachers, ordained pastors, and gifted evangelists. Each one of us is called to know our faith and be able to explain and defend it (1 Peter 3:15). And, as we've seen in Paul's words to Titus, we who are older are instructed specifically to pass our knowledge of our God on to our younger sisters in the faith. On occasion, doing so may mean speaking up for what is right when no one else will.

When a friend was in the middle of an enormously unpleasant divorce, a couple who had been longtime friends came alongside her. The husband offered to escort my friend to some social gatherings. Although the relationship was purely platonic, she nevertheless asked this question at lunch one day: "Should I continue to attend public functions with him?" A very shy and usually very quiet woman spoke up without hesitation. "No," she said simply but firmly, "I believe our appearances and our actions should be above reproach." There was a holy hush in that room. It takes courage to speak forth words like those, and a person who clearly knows what she believes finds that courage.

A Loving Commitment to People

John D. Rockefeller once said, "I would pay any price for a man who was able to get along with others." Living in relationship, in harmony with the people around us, is not easy for us human beings. That's why Christian community can be such a testimony in our world. After all, didn't Jesus command us to love one another (Mark 12:31)? And doesn't the Bible teach that people will know us as God's people by our love for one another (John 13:35)? Such love means standing by difficult people, staying with someone for the long haul, and asking God to give us hearts that accept the people we encounter and eyes to see Jesus in them. Being in relationship with people means being a channel of God's grace in the world.

A Willingness to Extend Warm Hospitality

My Aunt Pat was one of the most influential people in my life. She didn't finish high school, and she never held more than a part-time waitressing job in the dining room of a private law association. Aunt Pat's influence came not from a fine education or a powerful, prestigious position. Her influence on me came as she cooked, sewed, baked, and served her church and her community. Her influence came as she personified hospitality.

Every time I went to Aunt Pat's home, a wonderful smell from the kitchen greeted me—lemon pound cake, freshly baked bread, the spices of Assyrian food. The table in her kitchen table often had on it a huge floral tablecloth, and it didn't matter who you were or what time of day or night you arrived. She made everyone feel welcome and accepted. Within minutes, you had something to eat or drink in your hand despite the fact that in those days my aunt and uncle didn't know anything about "extra" money in a bank account. Dear Aunt Pat made me want to cook, bake, crochet, embroider, be hospitable, love others—in a word, imitate her. She was a model, a messenger, an older woman God placed in my life to help me enter adulthood. Her lessons about the value of hospitality went straight to my heart.

Availability, Acceptance, and Affirmation

A classic example of an older woman being there for a younger woman in a Titus 2 relationship is found in the relationship between Elizabeth and Mary. Where did young Mary go when she learned from the angel that she, a virgin engaged to be married, was carrying God's Son in her womb? She went straight to her older cousin Elizabeth. Now remember that in her day Mary could have been stoned for being pregnant. At the very least she could be ostracized and cast away. What would happen to her planned marriage? Would Joseph believe her account of the angel and God's message? Clearly, these early days of pregnancy may not have been very comfortable or easy for Mary for a variety of emotional as well as physical reasons. So Mary went to Elizabeth, and Elizabeth received her warmly. Elizabeth was lovingly available, she wholeheartedly accepted and welcomed her cousin (just as the cartwheeling baby in her own womb welcomed the baby in Mary's!), and she affirmed the wondrous privilege Mary had of being chosen by God for a special purpose.

Availability, acceptance, and affirmation—a woman of God can give these to another woman. Other people in her life can be critics—she needs a cheerleader. Others can try to force her toward their goals for her—she needs to be loved for who she is and what she dreams. Others can be busy with their own things—she wants someone who will simply spend some time with her. Others will be too busy talking to ever listen—she needs someone eager to hear her. Other women might try to make her a mirror image of themselves—she needs a woman who will help her become the person God has called her to be. In fact, that's one of the primary motives of a godly woman who walks alongside another woman.

> I spoke
> Words fell
> Aimlessly on ears.
> Later
> One said,
> "Your word—
> It helped
> That day."
>
> I turned
> Wondering—
> Forgot I said
> That word.
> Let me speak
> Those words
> Often.
> Helpful words
> That I forget.
>
> —Jim Elliot in The Journals of Jim Elliot

A heart for God, a teachable spirit, the Lord's perspective on time, a solid knowledge of their faith, the ability and boldness to share their beliefs, a commitment to people, a warm hospitality for all who come their way, a loving availability, and an accepting, affirming spirit—these are the traits of the woman of God, the Titus woman, the older woman who can make a difference for God's kingdom by passing on His truth and His values to the next generation. What motivates such a woman to draw alongside another woman, a younger woman? She doesn't do it to earn another jewel in her crown. She's not seeking a substitute daughter or trying to clone herself. She's not opting for an easy "out" when it comes to serving God. (This ministry can, in fact, be as costly as it is rewarding!) No, a godly woman is simply acting out of obedience to God's clearly stated command in Titus 2. She is giving away what she has and who she is, she is imparting God's truth and extending fond affection, she is being Jesus with skin and bones to the women to whom God calls her to reach out.

As I've studied Titus 2 and listened for God's direction, I've been guided by the words of Elisabeth Elliot Gren: "God ordained that I participate." God ordained this older woman/younger woman relationship—these blessed relationships between women of God—so that you and I would participate. Elisabeth helped me see that God does His work and I am to do mine. The Lord doesn't say, "I hope you follow My plan." He says, "Follow it!"

Is your life in order so that you can obey? Are you listening for God's specific instructions to you? Is your heart open so that you will hear where He leads and then go where He directs? His commandment is issued to you— and His blessings await when you respond!

Epilogue

Our Privilege

It was Sunday morning. As we've done every week for four years, my husband and I went to our classroom at church to teach the 50 faithful couples who attend Family Circles. These bright, educated young men and women love God, one another, and us.

But this Sunday was not a typical one. Less than 24 hours earlier my husband's father had died at the age of 88. When David and I discussed whether we should go to class, we decided the best place for us to be was at the house of God with people who love Him as we do.

As David stood before the men and women who had prayed with us and for us through the 12 months of Poppa Otto's decline, he described the previous 24 hours, Poppa's strained breathing, his last minutes, and plans for his final resting place.

When David finished, a young man rose to his feet and said, "Could a few men gather around David and pray for him?" I will never forget that image of not a few but all of the men in the class rising quickly and surrounding David. Tears filled my eyes as I saw these men honor their father in the faith. Their fervent prayers revealed their love, concern, and respect for David. Later in the day, David told me it took all of his physical strength to stand erect under the force of the men's hands on his shoulders. What a powerful reminder of God's love!

And those reminders continued in the days that followed as these dear young friends sent cards and flowers, brought meals, attended the memorial service, ran errands, drove us to the airport—did anything they could to demonstrate their love and support. David and I were very touched and very blessed.

I couldn't help but think of what God said to Ruth when he gave her a son: "May he also be to you a restorer of life and a sustainer of your old age" (Ruth 4:15). These sons and daughters in the faith certainly were restoring and sustaining us. I also thought of Jesus' words—"Behold, My mother and My brothers! For whoever does the will of My Father who is in heaven, he is My brother and sister and mother" (Matthew 12:49,50). These dear young friends are indeed family, and David and I thank God for them.

Family Duty, Family Privilege

Prepared to read a passage of Scripture and say a few words at the memorial service for her grandfather, our daughter Anissa stood at the podium. When she saw the number of young faces in the congregation, her first words were "I'm an only daughter who lives away from her parents. I know that it is you who comfort and care for my parents. Thank you."

With that simple statement, David and I realized that the young men and women in our world—in Family

Circles, in Mentors for Moms, in Homemakers by Choice, and in Study Sisters—are the sons and daughters of our heart. They are indeed God's family—our family—and they do, as Anissa recognized, support and care for us in a multitude of ways. And that's exactly what our heavenly Father planned for us. As His family, we are to care for one another.

And one way we older members of the family care for younger members (and even our peers) is by sharing with them our knowledge of God and His Word. Just as each generation of Israel declared to the next the faithfulness of God through accounts of the Passover, the Red Sea parting, the exodus from Egypt, the manna sent from heaven, the guiding cloud by day and the blazing fire by night, we who are the new Israel—God's children, heirs with Christ—are to share our own testimonies of His faithfulness.

In my 50 years of living, I have indeed seen God be faithful—again and again, in the big things and the little things, in my life and in the lives of others. And this witness is an important gift for us to give to other believers, and perhaps especially to younger people struggling with the challenges of life which we have already faced. It is so important that, as we have seen in our study of Titus 2, God commands that we do so. Look again at God's call to you:

> Older women likewise are to be reverent in their behavior, not malicious gossips, nor enslaved to much wine, teaching what is good, that they may encourage

the young women to love their husbands, to love their children, to be sensible, pure, workers at home, kind, being subject to their own husbands, that the word of God may not be dishonored (Titus 2:3-5).

Being a Titus 2 woman, a spiritual mother, a beacon of God's love takes time and energy. It means risk. It calls you to be vulnerable and open. So why do it? Because God commands it and so "that the word of God will not be dishonored." You know God and His Word. To not share that hard-won, lifelong knowledge would indeed dishonor Him and His truth. Furthermore, the hours, the energy, the prayer, the love you invest in some of God's precious daughters will not only please the King of kings, but it will also mean a great blessing for you as you draw closer to these members of His family.

Obedience, Joy, and Blessing

God commands. God calls. And when He calls, He equips. There's no reason for any of us to hold back from the Titus 2 ministry which is part of the Good Lord's plan. So be a doer of the Word, not just a hearer (James 1:22)— but don't wait too long! (Remember the virgins in Matthew 25:1-10 who didn't have their lamps ready and, as a result, missed the wedding feast when the bridegroom came?)

You and I certainly have the freedom to say no to God. We do so all the time. But don't say no! Don't miss the blessing! God's Titus 2 design, His older woman-younger woman plan, is intended to bless you as much as it blesses your sisters in the faith. (In fact, on occasion, I'm sure I've been far more blessed than my daughter of the heart!)

So accept God's call. Respond to His call to this special ministry with prayer, with His love for the woman He sends your way, and with the confidence that He will use you whatever your strengths and weaknesses, whatever your joys and struggles, whatever your story, whatever your dreams.

Don't underestimate how God will use you or the gifts He has given you to share. Instead, love the way you can love—with encouragement, perspective, and wisdom. That kind of love is just what your sisters in Christ—whatever their age—need and want!

Furthermore, your obedience will mean joy and blessing beyond expectation. As you pass on the passions of your life and the convictions of your heart, you will indeed be blessed at the same time that the Lord uses you to bless one of His precious daughters. It is my prayer that, as you minister in this crucial and life-changing way, you will join with Paul in saying,

> *Having thus a fond affection for you, we were well-pleased to impart to you not only the gospel of God but also our own lives.*
> —1 Thessalonians 2:8

Appendix

Mentors for Moms

"Please sing it again, Grandma Sybil!" the little boy said into the telephone. And she gladly did:

> *Two little eyes to look to God*
> *Two little ears to hear His Word*
> *Two little feet to walk His ways*
> *Two little lips to sing His praise*
> *Two little hands to do His will*
> *And one little heart to love Him still.*

"Grandma Sybil" is an honorary title. Despite the obvious mutual affection, she's not related to this little boy by blood. Instead, she is an older woman of God who has taken seriously His command in Titus 2 and responded by joining Mentor for Moms, a program I founded five years ago. She is now a mentor for a young mom, who has truly become a daughter of the heart.

Now mentors in my program aren't required to know the words to children's songs (and the hand gestures that go along), but they are required to know the Word of God—but most of our mentors know both! Grandma Sybil knows the right kind of songs for her daughter of the heart's young son, and she also knows the Word of God and what it has for daughters of the heart today. Mentors for Moms brings older women like Sybil together with younger moms in a Titus 2 relationship. Let me tell you more about the program.

Mentors for Moms: An Overview

Since all my life I have been so strongly and so positively influenced by the older women God has placed along my path, I deeply desired to find a way to help other young women experience the rich blessings of such relationships. My home church—Scottsdale Bible Church in Arizona—seemed the best place to start. So in 1991, Joan Malouf and I put our heads together, drafted a proposal, consulted with our church staff, and began Mentors for Moms. (We're pleased that the program—whose title was quickly shortened to "M4Ms" and whose trademark instantly became snacking on M&Ms—now has a permanent place in the courses offered the women of our church each year.)

The purpose of the program? To give young women the opportunity to hear and be encouraged by an older woman's godly perspective on life. And, defined from the other side, to give older women the opportunity to respond to God's call to ministry in Titus 2. By now, you know the mandate:

Older women likewise are to be reverent in their behavior, not malicious gossips, not enslaved to much wine, teaching what is good, that they may encourage the young women to love their husbands, to love their children, to be sensible, pure, workers at home, kind, being subject to their own husbands, that the Word of God may not be dishonored (Titus 2:3-5).

The program gives older women a plan for such a ministry so that she can indeed be a blessing to a young woman in the very areas Paul outlines.

As I studied these three verses from Titus, I saw God calling us older women to model and encourage younger women in four different areas of life, and the following outline evolved:

I. My Own Life
   a. Kindness
   b. Pureness
   c. Sensibleness

II. My Mate
   a. Loving to my husband
   b. Subject to my husband

III. My Children
   a. Loving to my children

IV. My Home
   a. Being a "keeper of the home"

From these four points came 24 weeks of teaching that address these Titus 2:3-5 areas. The M4M curriculum class titles are listed here:

I. My Own Life
"The Character of a Christian"
"You Are What You Say"
"Why Stay Home?—or You Are the Best
   Choice"
"Disciplines of a Godly Woman"
"Purity in the Woman of the '90s"
"Be an Imitator"

II. My Mate
"The Way to Your Husband's Heart"
"Building Your Mate in Love"
"Communicating with Your Mate"
"How to Love Your Husband"
"Simply Submit"
"Intimacy"

III. My Children
"Diagnosing Your Child"
"Training the Will of Your Child—Part I"
"Training the Will of Your Child—Part II"
"Reality Discipline"
"The Ministry of Motherhood"
"Learning to Love Your Children"

IV. My Home
"The Ministry in My Mansion"
"Keepers of the Home"
"Food, Menus, and Hospitality"
"Finances and Budgets"
"Feathering Your Nest"
"Creating Memories in Your Home"

Each of these areas is important so that, in Paul's words, "the Word of God may not be dishonored" (Titus 2:5) by the way we women—old and young alike—live our daily lives.

The lead M4M teacher presents the material listed above to an audience of twosomes, each comprised of an older woman and a young mother. These pairs offer each other the accountability, sharing, authenticity, confidentiality, and prayer support found in a typical church small group. As some of the letters found in chapter 10 reflect, the program has been well accepted, and women of all ages have benefited greatly.

The Role of Prayer

One of the significant elements in this God-ordained relationship between a younger woman and an older woman is the older woman's faithful prayers for her mom. No one can know the vital role such prayer plays in the older woman's ministry and the younger woman's struggles.

Praying for her young woman's walk with the Lord, her need for His protection, and her ability to hear His voice keeps the mentor mindful of her major goals and the bigger issues of a young woman's life. Of course the older woman also prays about the specific and daily concerns her young mother talks about. And then there are those issues which are somewhat unique to the '90s. . . .

The Needs in the '90s

In 1990, I met a 30-year-old woman, an attorney with one child. She and her husband had just moved to Scottsdale from Oklahoma when she met a woman at a park who said, "Oh, yes! I'm a stay-at-home mom and I love it. Come hear our teacher."

After her first class with Mentors for Moms, this young woman came to me and said, "I'm thirty years old and I've never heard anyone tell me to stay at home. Not a single person!" Her parents, her education, her circle of friends, and certainly her work environment all said, "Work!" But she decided to ignore those voices. She became an active part of this young mothers' group and chose to stay at home and have another child. What fun to watch her grow as she felt encouraged and supported to do what God had told her!

And she's not the only mom who has found the support she needed in Mentors for Moms. I recently received a letter from a brand-new mom who said, "I am feeling a great deal of pressure to put my baby in the mom's morning out program or to at least give her a bottle instead of breastfeeding her so I can get some relief. Donna, I need help. I love being home, and I want my little girl to sleep in her own bed when she naps, not the car seat because her mom is running around. Please give me some assistance."

How I wish all my letters were so easy to respond to! I told her, without hesitation, "Yes, yes! A thousand times yes! Stay at home and care for your loved ones. You will never be sorry!" She knew what her heart was telling her to do. All she needed was affirmation—or, to use a '90s word, validation—for her choice. And older women like you and me—women who have raised their children—can offer that much-needed support to today's younger generation. These women are the most educated who have ever walked on the planet (most of them have a four-year college degree and some have postgraduate work), but they need you, the older woman, to affirm their difficult choice to stay at home with their children.

From what I see, women in the '90s also struggle with the closely related issues of commitment and responsibility. The young wife or mother who was raised in a broken home may struggle with what commitment looks like—"Can I make a commitment and keep it? Will my husband make commitments and keep them? How can I teach our children about commitment?" Responsibility is the ability to follow through on a commitment. It's saying "yes" to a project and then seeing it through to completion even when the task gets more difficult than anticipated.

What evidence do I have that people of the '90s don't understand responsibility and commitment? Consider that the simple act of responding to an invitation's RSVP is a dying art. These days, parents of the bride are aghast at the poor response to formal wedding invitations. Even more troublesome are the individuals who responsibly call and say "yes" but then do not attend! They don't follow through on their commitment; they don't complete the task. Trained differently than the '90s woman was, the older woman understands commitment and responsibility, she knows the importance of fulfilling obligations, and she can pass this knowledge on to a young wife and mom. Commitment and responsibility, simple courtesy and basic good manners—these are simple but important gifts that older women can pass on to their younger counterparts. And that's some of what happens in Mentors for Moms.

Here is how Sherilyn Jameson, one young mom in Mentors for Moms, summed up the situation:

Where Have All the Mentors Gone?

Where have all the mentors gone—
Those Titus 2 women of the past,
Those older, God-fearing role models?
Where have all the mentors gone?

Maybe you've gone to seek fulfilling careers.
Maybe you've gone to self-awareness classes.
Maybe you're busy staying fit—playing tennis or
*   at aerobics.*
Or maybe you're just taking time for yourselves—
Going to lunch, playing bridge, or shopping at
*   the mall.*

Wherever you have gone, we've missed you.
Our generation has indeed missed you.
We need you.
Maybe more than any generation of mothers.
With our vague role descriptions and society's
*   confusing messages,*
Oh, how we need faithful, committed mentors.

We need you to remind us of the value of being a stay-at-home mom and a loyal, submissive wife.

We need to see the art of homemaking modeled for us over and over and over again.

We need to listen to the advice of an older woman now that we know what to listen for.

We need to watch you respond to the joy and sorrow of life, with the divine wisdom of God's Word;
we need to see how God's promises in Scripture work out in real life.

We need your encouragement to see the eternal picture and the benefits of following God
when the day is bogging us down
and clouding our view.

We need your tried-and-true tips
on loving our husband, raising our children,
keeping our home, and living for Jesus.

We need to listen and learn from the wealth
of experience and wisdom you've collected
during your years of living.

We need you cheering us on when
it seems no one is noticing or appreciating
our many efforts to make
our houses homes,
our children saints for the King,

our husband our top priority,
and Jesus the love of our life.

We need to hear your many little comments
that remind us that this exhausting stage
in our life is indeed a stage and it is temporary.

We need, possibly more than anything else,
a mentor in our life
who will take our name before the Father daily,
beseeching His throne on our behalf.

Where have all the mentors gone?
You may have gone many different places.
But we know where a few of you are—
involved with Mentors for Moms.

—Sherilyn Jameson

Other Lessons for Life

During the years that I've watched older and younger women come together in Mentors for Moms, I've also seen young moms benefit from lessons older women have learned about the pain and suffering that life brings. I know that, a few years ago, when we moved my 87-year-old father-in-law into our home, I looked for a woman who had already walked through the last years of her parents' lives. I subscribed to *Parent Advisor* and read articles on caring for the aged and the children's role in a parent's life. But what helped most were the words of women who had lived through what I was now experiencing, who had watched a physically strong man undergo the attacks of Alzheimer's disease and be left sadly confused, who knew the whole gamut of emotions—uprootedness, helplessness, frustration, sadness—that I was feeling.

As I think back on that time when Poppa was in our home, I must also mention the invaluable help I received from two daughters of my heart during this difficult season. Cliffy came to our home for a month, and five days a week she was available to help me. Jen also came alongside to do for me what I couldn't do for myself at that time. I will always be grateful to these dear young women who were by my side lightening the load when the days were long and hard.

Whether we're young or old, it's easier to deal with life's hard times when we don't go it alone—and that's what a Titus 2 ministry is all about. An older woman can keep a younger woman from having to go it alone by being there with her. The older woman can also offer reassurance that she's a kindred spirit, that she knows pain, and, often, that she's experienced the same circumstances. A difficult pregnancy, a miscarriage, the death of a child, financial struggles, a job loss, a family crisis, marital problems—these things and more bring us pain. And when pain comes to a younger woman, an older woman can be available, willing to listen, and willing to walk alongside her. She can also, when the moment is right, offer the perspective that God uses life's hard times to draw us close to Him, refine our faith, and make us more like Christ. I've found that, if an older woman is one who blesses, she is one who has experienced the hardest of life and has learned the value of trials and joy in the midst of them. She has clung to the words of 1 Peter 1:6,7 ("In this you greatly rejoice, even though now for a little while, if necessary, you have been distressed by various trials, that the proof of your faith, being more precious than gold which is perishable, even though tested by fire, may be found to result in praise and glory and honor at the revelation of Jesus Christ"), and now she can offer that same hope to the younger woman who is hurting.

Passing on this wisdom, sharing her love of God, and testifying to His faithfulness and goodness is what an older woman is called to do. God commands us to pass on His ways to the next generation. When the Navajo people neglected that duty, American cowboy artist Ray Swanson stepped in and, through his painting, preserved art forms of the Navajo culture. He is an example to us as we share the art and culture of becoming godly women, building a marriage that glorifies God, caring for our children as God would have us do, and making our home a peaceful place that welcomes people in the Lord's name. This entails much that is mundane (ironing shirts, setting the table, preparing meals, changing diapers, scrubbing toilets—you know the list!), but even in that an older woman can help and be a beacon of God's light when she does. After all, how often, when you were a young homemaker, did you struggle with a recipe only to have an older, more experienced woman say, "Here! Try this! It's easy and delicious!" We older women can do the same thing for our younger woman's life outside the kitchen—for her spiritual life, her marriage, her mothering, and her homemaking. Indeed, what a privilege!

"That I Can Do!"

Marie Peterson, wife of composer/musician John W. Peterson and a fellow church member, has always kept a low profile. By choice, she has stayed out of the limelight. Through the years, I've occasionally asked her to sit on a panel or let me interview her. I'd receive a polite but firm "no" after which she would often add, "I don't have anything to say. I've always been John's wife and the girls' mother—nothing more, nothing less." Despite the fact that those tasks are incredibly important and she did an above average job, Marie did not feel called to speak publicly.

Well, when Mentors for Moms began, I went to her again and asked her to be involved. This time her response was a hearty "Yes! That I can do!"—and she did a wonderful job. The fortunate young mother who had Marie as her older woman will be blessed all her life by Marie's godly and rich perspective on living in a way that glorifies God.

So you don't fancy yourself a Marie? Then think of Grandma Sybil. Remember her little song? Even if that's all she'd had to give, I'm confident that—as she said, "Here I am" in obedience to God and as she entered into this special Titus 2 relationship—she would have trusted Him that it was enough to give. So if you feel you don't have much to give, I say to you, "Trust God, as many older women before you have, that what He's given you—even if it's 'just' a children's song and a desire to obey Him—is enough for you to do the ministry He's called you to." When God calls, He empowers and in that little book of Titus He's clearly calling you to pass on to the next generation your love for Him and your knowledge of His ways.

Find Us Faithful

We're pilgrims on the journey
Of the narrow road
And those who've gone before us line the way
Cheering on the faithful, encouraging the weary
Their lives a stirring testament to God's sustaining
    grace.

Surrounded by so great a cloud of witnesses
Let us run the race not only for the prize
But as those who've gone before us
Let us leave to those behind us
The heritage of faithfulness passed on
    through godly lives.

Oh may all who come behind us find us faithful
May the fire of our devotion light their way
May the footprints that we leave
Lead them to believe
And the lives we live inspire them to obey
Oh may all who come behind us find us faithful.

After all our hopes and dreams have come and gone
And our children sift through all we've left behind
May the clues that they discover and the memories
    they uncover

*Become the light that leads them to the road we
each must find.*

*Oh may all who come behind us find us faithful
May the fire of our devotion light their way
May the footprints that we leave
Lead them to believe
And the lives we live inspire them to obey.*

*Oh may all who come behind us find us faithful
May the fire of our devotion light their way
May the footprints that we leave
Lead them to believe
And the lives we live inspire them to obey
Oh may all who come behind us find us faithful.*

For information on
Mentors for Moms
write:
Donna Otto
11453 North 53rd Place
Scottsdale, AZ 85254

Study Guide

A Personal Journey

Grab a pen and notepad for this part!

Chapter 1: The Classroom of the Heart

꙳ In an average week, how much time do you spend with other women? Where do you see them? What do you do when you're together? What do you especially enjoy about friendships and contact with other women?

꙳ In a sentence or two, state your reaction to God's commands to you in Titus 2:3-5.

꙳ Do you have an Aunt Pat? If so, how have you been blessed by your Aunt Pat? If not, what would you have appreciated receiving from such an older woman?

꙳ Are you an Aunt Pat to someone? Are you giving her what your Aunt Pat gave you or what you would have wanted an Aunt Pat to give you? More importantly, are you giving her what God would have you give and what she needs?

Chapter 2: Is It Time for Me?

꙳ Do you seek out younger women? Why or why not? If

so, what kind of relationships with younger women do you currently enjoy? What kind of relationship with younger women do you most enjoy?

∾ How do you feel about aging? What thoughts do you have about this inevitable and God-ordained process? What is the root of the majority of your thoughts and feelings, positive or negative? How would you respond to this poem?

I Shall Not Mind

I shall not mind
The whiteness of my hair
Or that slow steps falter
On the stair,
Or what strange image
Greets me in the glass—
If I can feel,
As roots feel in the sod,
That I am growing old to bloom
Before the face of God.

—Author unknown

∾ List ten things you can offer a younger woman. Let "perspective" start off your list.

Chapter 3: The Value of Vulnerability

∾ To what current situation or concern in your life does the statement "Fear not" or "Be not afraid" speak? If the words seem just words, spend a few minutes in prayer and ask God to help you hear them as His specific message to you.

∽ What do you think of when you hear the word *risk?* What risk have you recently taken? Comment on the outcome and what you learned from that experience. What risk did you recently bypass? Comment on what you learned from that choice.

∽ What about your life and yourself do you find risky to share? What will you look for in a confidante? When you do feel ready to share, pray about your upcoming conversation, and then "Be not afraid"! Taking the risk of being vulnerable and sharing ourselves builds bridges between us and other people that can't otherwise be built.

Chapter 4: Between Women of God

∽ When you have an opportunity to get to know someone, what interferes with your attempts to make a new friend? What can you do to remove these roadblocks?

∽ For a less-threatening getting-to-know-you exercise, ask that potential new friend the following questions.

- What are five of your all-time favorite books?
- What are two of your favorite movies?
- What are the topics of two of your favorite sermons?

∾ What makes listening difficult for you? If listening comes rather easily for you, thank God for that gift. If you want to be a better listener, make that a matter of prayer.

Chapter 5: Daughters of the Heart

∾ What do you most enjoy about your current prayer life? What can you do to improve your prayer life, to increase and/or enhance your communication with your heavenly Father and His Son, your Savior and Lord? What will be your first step toward that improved prayer life, and when will you take that step?

∾ What topic in Scripture would you like to explore more thoroughly? What will be the first three steps you will take toward learning more about this topic, and when will you start? Could you and your younger woman learn together?

Chapter 6: A Touch of Grace

∾ When has someone been God-with-skin-and-bones to you? Talk about this person's impact on your life.

∾ Are you an "available woman"? Why or why not?

∾ Who are the significant women in your life? What do you admire about them?

∾ How do you feel about the state of our society and your responsibility to the next generation?

Chapter 7: Caught in Comparison

∾ What comparisons between yourself and other women do you find yourself making most often? Why do you think you are especially sensitive about that/those trait(s)?

∾ What can you do to change your habit of making comparisons? What does God's Word say to you about your value to Him, your Creator? How can God's Word and His Spirit help you change your pattern of thinking about yourself? What is the first step you will take toward freedom from comparing yourself to others?

∾ Complete the following statements about yourself. Let this exercise help you appreciate the unique and wonderful creation you are.

I am a

I wonder

I hear

I see

I want

I am

I pretend

I feel

I touch

I worry

I cry

I am

I understand

I say

I dream

I try

I hope

I am

Chapter 8: A Unique Way of Giving

∾ If you have been blessed with a daughter, write her a note telling her how very special she is to you.

∾ In the Old Testament, the suffering Job said of God, "Though he slay me, yet will I trust in him" (Job 13:15 KJV). How well do you do when it comes to trusting God? What verse or two from the Bible help strengthen your faith when it wavers?

∾ Think back on a time when you found comfort under God's wings. What did that experience teach you about God? How did it strengthen your trust in Him?

Chapter 9: Frustrations and Farewells

∾ We are called to be stewards of our time as well as our

treasures and our talents. How are you spending your days? What does last week's calendar reveal about your priorities? What good things did you do? What better things could you have been doing?

∾ In what area of your life do you most struggle with setting boundaries? Why do you struggle with setting boundaries? To whom can you go for support (prayer and practical) and accountability?

∾ How do you usually respond to someone who is slow to catch on to what you are saying or teaching? How would you like to respond to a slow student? How would Jesus want you to respond—and how can He help you do so?

∾ When has someone you love moved away? What feelings did you have when you said good-bye, and how did you deal with them?

Chapter 10: Rave Reviews

∾ Write a letter to God and tell Him what you hear as His call to you personally in Titus 2, your concerns about responding to that call, and your hopes for a ministry of coming alongside a woman of God to share your knowledge of Him. Let this letter be a prayer as well as a touchstone for you in the future when you are being a Titus 2 woman.

Chapter 11: The Fingerprint of God

❧ Read the verses that follow. How do they encourage you in your walk with the Lord?

- When Thou didst say, "Seek My face," my heart said to Thee, "Thy face, O LORD, I shall seek" (Psalm 27:8).

- And I will give them a heart to know Me, for I am the LORD; and they will be My people, and I will be their God, for they will return to Me with their whole heart (Jeremiah 24:7).

- As for you, my son Solomon, know the God of your father, and serve Him with a whole heart and a willing mind; for the LORD searches all hearts, and understands every intent of the thoughts. If you seek Him, He will let you find Him . . . (1 Chronicles 28:9).

- The young lions do lack and suffer hunger; but they who seek the LORD shall not be in want of any good thing (Psalm 34:10).

❧ How do you think you can cultivate the traits listed in this chapter?

Thank you for sharing your journey with me!